SHE SAID / HE SAID:

AN ANNOTATED BIBLIOGRAPHY OF SEX DIFFERENCES IN LANGUAGE, SPEECH, AND NONVERBAL COMMUNICATION

Compiled by Nancy Henley and Barrie Thorne

KNOW, inc.

FREEDOM OF THE PRESS BELONGS
TO THOSE WHO OWN THE PRESS!

P.O. Box 86031 • Pittsburgh, Pa. 15221

FIRST KNOW EDITION DECEMBER, 1975

First published as Bibliography of:
    LANGUAGE AND SEX: DIFFERENCE AND DOMINANCE
    by Barrie Thorne and Nancy Henley, Newbury House, Rowley,
    Mass.
KNOW, INC.,
P.O. Box 86031, Pittsburgh, PA 15221
ISBN 0-912786-36-1

PREFACE

An Annotated Bibliography

The history of this bibliography reflects the recent burgeoning of interest in the relationship of language and sex. We began compiling the bibliography in 1972, thinking that it would be a modest venture since so few researchers had taken account of the sexual differentation of language, although linguists and others had long been aware of the linguistic consequences of class, race, social setting, and political relations. Often when sex *was* considered in the study of language, it was defined as a curiosity and a source of amusement.

This situation began to change with the emergence of the women's liberation movement in the late 1960's. Feminists saw the importance of language as an institution which helps shape people's lives, and they called attention to the sexism which is deeply rooted in language structure and use. The women's movement began to spur interest in these issues in more academic quarters, especially among women researchers. Linguists, lexicographers, speech physiologists, psychologists, sociologists, anthropologists, literary critics, and people in speech communication, education, and English literature have all begun examining the sexual differentiation of language.

This recent spurt of interest accounts for many of the bibliography items. In this edition (the fourth since we first began informally distributing the bibliography in July, 1973) there are 81 items about language differences dated after 1970, 34 items dated between 1961-70, 12 from 1951-60, and 20 from the first 50 years of the century. The entries in the bibliography represent a wide range of disciplines and methods of study. This convergence of disciplines holds many possibilities for future breakthroughs and for the raising of new questions and perspectives.

Each item in the bibliography is annotated and arranged by topic; the topics cover various dimensions of language and nonverbal communication. One basic distinction is between language *about* the sexes (included under section II-A, "Sexist Bias of English Language"), and differences in the way women and men *use* language (differences in word choice, syntactic usage, and language style; phonology; conversational patterns; speech in multilingual situations; language acquisition; verbal ability). A final section, on sex differences in nonverbal communication, is intended to raise the issue of the interrelationship between verbal and nonverbal behavior. We have not tried to make this section comprehensive.

Some of the items are annotated or referred to under more than one topic. This cross referencing is indicated in brackets at the end of the annotation. An index to the bibliography, arranged by author, is also included. Where papers are unpublished, we have tried, where possible, to provide the address of the author(s). Italics and brackets indicate our comments as editors, sometimes providing cross references, and at other points providing asides, criticisms, reminders, and explanatory discussions.

We would like to acknowledge assistance from the Department of Sociology, Michigan State University, which made possible early informal circulation of the bibliography. We are also grateful to people from all over the country who have called our attention to references we had missed, sent us copies of their papers, shared information with us, and generally been most supportive. Mary Ritchie Key and Cheris Kramer have been particularly helpful. A spirit of sisterhood has made work on the bibliography a special pleasure.

DEDICATION

To our sisters . . .

Edyth and Dottie   Sandra and Avril

"Women are hearing each other and ourselves for the first
time, and out of this supportive hearing emerge new words."

Mary Daly

SHE SAID / HE SAID:

AN ANNOTATED BIBLIOGRAPHY OF
SEX DIFFERENCES IN LANGUAGE, SPEECH,
AND NONVERBAL COMMUNICATION

Compiled by Nancy Henley and Barrie Thorne

CONTENTS

INTRODUCTION

This bibliography, which began as a modest effort to pull together what we thought were very few published sources on language and sex, grew very rapidly to reach its present size. Part of the growth was due to the uncovering of sources buried in a wide range of places, and often not directly billed as dealing with this topic. For example, experimental psychologists have often used sex as a variable (mainly because it's an obvious, discrete way to categorize subjects), and among their findings are some bearing on this subject. Much of the growth of the bibliography, however, is due to the increased attention which this general topic is receiving; the reader might note that by far the bulk of references are dated since the late 1960's, that is, since the inception of the women's liberation movement.

Our goal has been to compile this information in the most useful form possible. Each item is annotated and arranged by topic. The topics include various dimensions of language and nonverbal communication; this is only one of several alternative ways of organizing this information. One important distinction is between language *about* the sexes (included under II-A, "Sexist Bias of English Language"), and differences in the way women and men *use* language (differences in word choice, syntactic usage, and language style; phonology; conversational patterns; speech in multilingual situations; language acquisition; verbal ability). A final section, on sex differences in nonverbal communication, does not claim to be comprehensive; it is included to raise the issue of the interrelationship between verbal and nonverbal behavior, and to break down the artificial isolation of speech from other modes of communication.

Some of the items are annotated or referred to under more than one topic. This cross referencing is indicated in brackets at the end of the annotation. An index to the bibliography, arranged by author, is also included. Where papers are unpublished, we have tried, where possible, to provide the address of the author(s). Italics and brackets indicate that the editors are commenting, sometimes providing cross references, and at other points providing asides, criticisms, reminders, and explanatory discussions.

I. COMPREHENSIVE SOURCES: LANGUAGE AND SPEECH

BODINE, ANN.
"Sex Differentiation in Language." In Barrie Thorne and Nancy Henley, eds., *Language and Sex: Difference and Dominance.* Rowley, Mass.: Newbury House, 1975.

Bodine reviews the history of the study of sex differentiation in language, offers a comprehensive analysis of the various forms sex differentiation takes in a wide variety of languages, and reviews the attitudes of the speakers and the linguists toward linguistic sex differentiation. Sex differentiation may be *sex-exclusive* (forms used exclusively by one sex) or *sex-preferential* (forms differing in frequency of occurrence in speech of women and men), and has been generally discussed under separate topics of gender and "women's language." Earlier linguists (1) generally failed to see any connection between gender in language (assignment of sex to certain forms) and sex differentiation of other types; (2) took the notion of gender for granted, but marveled at descriptions of (presumably) sex-exclusive differentiation in far-off cultures; (3) ignored the evidence of sex-preferential speech in their own European languages, though (4) they thought that in their own languages women spoke differently; and (5) generally equated "men's language" (including their own) with *the* language. Chatterji, for example, equated Bengali language with men's speech, stating that the initial *l-* is often pronounced as *n-* by women, children, and the uneducated—who must constitute the great bulk of Bengali speakers. Obviously the difference might be represented otherwise, perhaps better, by the statement that "initial *n-* is sometimes pronounced *as l-* in pretentious speech, particularly that of status-conscious men." Bodine develops a classificatory scheme of axes: (1) type of language differences (pronunciation, form—acoustic and prosodic differences are omitted), and (2) the basis of language difference (sex of speaker, spoken to, speaker plus spoken to, or spoken about), and reviews the literature describing sex differences for each category of the classification. Differences based on sex of *speaker,* in both pronunciation and form, are remarkably superficial, nor is there profound difference in syntactic patterning. With regard to sex of *spoken to,* it seems to be a linguistic universal that no language differentiates on this basis which doesn't also differentiate on the basis of sex of speaker (excepting in direct address). Differentiation based on both *speaker and spoken to* could produce four versions, but no language with all four is known. There are no reports of pronunciation differences based on sex of *spoken about,* but differences in form on this basis are common (e.g., gender). The discussion of attitudes toward sex differentiation involves speakers' awareness of the differences; reports are often spotty with regard to whether both sexes are aware of the differences and/or can reproduce them. Ethnographers, generally male, tended to associate with male informants and may have given biased reports on attitudes toward sex differentiation in language. Descriptions of linguistic sex differentiation are uneven and incomplete for all languages, and the social implications are even less explored, though the present explosion of investigations (at least in English), concurrent with interest in social questions, suggests we may soon have a good understanding of sex differentiation in English. For a full understanding of sociolinguistic processes and regularities, however, a broad cross-cultural base is necessary. [*See V.*]

CONKLIN, NANCY FAIRES.
   "Toward a Feminist Analysis of Linguistic Behavior." *The University of Michigan Papers in Women's Studies,* 1, No. 1 (1974), 51-73.

   Conklin examines "various ways in which languages set women apart as a distinct group and how women set themselves apart." She surveys sex-marking in various languages in the form of specific words, endings, distinctions embedded in kinship systems, politeness-marking systems, taboos circumscribing women's use of speech, and in the speech genres and vocabularies specific to each sex. When the speech forms of men and women merge, change is usually in the direction of women adopting male language. Conklin discusses the pronoun system, the subtleties of sexist use of language, and the question of how each sex learns appropriate speech forms. Dialect studies reveal patterns of female speech: "hypercorrectness, respect for and acquiescence to 'standard' speech, judgments of persons' value and status on the basis of their accents, standardness, and style of speaking." Overall, Conklin argues, women have "acute sociolinguistic sensitivity," which entails being attuned to the behavior of others and relying on external norms. As a result, women may allow themselves to be defined by standards not necessarily their own; they may become alienated from their own culture and from other women. "But women's sensitivity to the behavior of others could be turned into a powerful tool for their liberation." There are strengths in female skill in manipulating language, in having a "large range of stylistic repertoires," in "attentiveness to what others are saying." "Both in dealing with the power structure, and in dealing with other women, an awareness of the ebb and flow below the surface of the interaction is a useful tool and also a valuable weapon." [See *II-A-2, II-B, IV-C, V, VI.*]

JESPERSEN, OTTO.
"The Woman," Chapter XIII of *Language: Its Nature, Development and Origin.* London: Allen & Unwin, 1922, pp. 237-254.

Among traditional books on language, Jespersen's discussion is the only extensive treatment of sex differences. He draws on a variety of sources: old ethnographies, novels, statements by Cicero and Lord Chesterfield, and makes many generalizations without even that sort of supporting evidence. Jespersen covers the following topics: (1) Ethnographic studies indicating that there are tribes in which men and women "speak totally different languages, or at any rate distinct dialects." These include differences in vocabulary, word taboos, and some grammatical forms unique to each sex. Jespersen suggests that these differences may be traced to the separate activities and roles of the sexes and to differences in rank. (2) The attitude of each sex toward language change. Jespersen presents a mixed picture: some believe women are more conservative than men with regard to language change, and that innovations are due to the initiative of men (he cites a source claiming that in France and England, women avoid coining new words; later, Jespersen himself asserts that "woman as a rule follows the main road of language, where man is often inclined to turn aside into a narrow footpath or even to strike out a new path for himself." On the other hand, he mentions a South American tribe where women "busied themselves in inventing new words," and a report that in Japan women are less conservative than men in pronunciation and in the selection of words and expressions. (3) Sex differences in phonetics. Although there are assorted examples of differences in pronunciation (e.g. women took the lead in weakening the old fully trilled tongue-point *r*), Jespersen claims that phonetically "there is scarcely any difference between the speech of men and that of women." (4) Choice of vocabulary and adverbs. Jespersen claims that women are more euphemistic than men, "instinctively" avoiding the coarseness of male speech. Men not only swear, but invent and use slang, and are more given to punning. The vocabulary of women, Jespersen claims, is less extensive than that of men, and women are more given to hyperbole, to adverbs of intensity. He claims that men use more complicated sentence constructions, building sentences "like a set of Chinese boxes," with clauses containing one within another. Women build sentences "like a string of pearls, joined together on a string of ands and similar words." Jespersen concludes with a barrage of generalizations, about "the greater rapidity of female thought" and the "superior readiness of the speech of women"–not "proof of intellectual power," but of talk without much prior thought ("a woman's thought is no sooner formed than uttered"). He attributes this to the domestic occupations of women which "demanded no deep thought, which were performed in company and could well be accompanied with a lively chatter." [See *II-B, V, VI.*]

KEY, MARY RITCHIE.
"Linguistic Behavior of Male and Female." *Linguistics,* 88 (Aug. 15, 1972), 15-31.

While linguists have dealt with dimensions of language variety such as age, socio-economic differences, and literary differences, they rarely discuss linguistic distinctions between the sexes. Sex differences in language may vary with group, situation, and role. Key summarizes findings by others and makes observations of her own about phonological differences in women's and men's speech, intonation patterns, male-female differences in syntax, the semantic component, and pronominal and nominal referents. [See II-A-1, II-B, III-B-3.]

KEY, MARY RITCHIE.
   Male/Female Language. Metuchen, N.J.: Scarecrow Press, 1975.

KRAMER, CHERIS.
   "Women's Speech: Separate But Unequal?" *Quarterly Journal of Speech,* 60 (Feb., 1974), 14-24. Reprinted in Barrie Thorne and Nancy Henley, eds., *Language and Sex: Difference and Dominance.* Rowley, Mass.: Newbury House, 1975.

   Kramer considers "evidence for there being systems of co-occurring, sex-linked linguistic signals in the United States" ("genderlects" or "sexlects"). She emphasizes the need to consider not only sex differences in grammar, phonology, and semantics, but also "possible differences in verbal skills, instrumental use of language, and the relationship of non-verbal uses to verbal behavior." Kramer reviews literature on male vs. female languages in primitive societies, and on phonetic differences between male and female speakers. She suggests the value of examining popular stereotypes about women's speech (how people think women speak or should speak), and from such stereotypes she draws out an imaginative list of research questions, e.g. on the relative verbosity of female vs. male speakers; patterns of question-asking; volume and pitch as they vary by situation; differences in the written work of men and women. Kramer hypothesizes that "women's speech reflects the stereotyped roles of male and female in our society, i.e., women in a subservient, nurturing position in a male-dominated world," although researchers should also be aware of differences among female speakers (related, for example, to differences of class, race, origin, age). Research into sex differences in speech should take account of the varied components of speech events [see Dell Hymes, "Models of Interaction of Language and Social Setting," Journal of Social Issues, XXXIII (1967), 8-28]: channel (oral, written, or other medium); key (tone, manner, or spirit of the act); setting or scene; participants (addressor, addressee, audience); topic; ends or purposes; norms of interaction; genres (categories or types of speech events, e.g. conversation, curse, lecture). [See II-B, III-A, III-B-2, IV-A, IV-C, VIII-C.]

LAKOFF, ROBIN.
   "Language and Woman's Place." *Language in Society,* 2 (1973), 45-79. Briefer version, "You Are What You Say," *Ms.,* 3 (July, 1974), 63-67. Also in the author's *Language and Woman's Place.* New York: Harper & Row, 1975.

   A lengthy paper which discusses two aspects of linguistic discrimination and prejudice against women: (1) The existence of a "woman's language," a style which avoids strong or forceful statements and encourages expressions that suggest triviality of subject matter, and uncertainty. Women are taught to use this special style of speech, which is later used against them in claims that women are unable to speak precisely, forcefully, or to take part in serious discussion. (2) General linguistic use which treats women as objects and defines them as secondary beings, having existence only when defined by a man. Lakoff uses data from her own speech and that of her acquaintances, and from the media. She concludes that language provides clues that some external situation needs changing, although social change creates lexical change, not the reverse. [See II-A-1, II-B, III-B-3, V, VII.]

THORNE, BARRIE AND NANCY HENLEY.
"Difference and Dominance: An Overview of Language, Gender, and Society." In Barrie Thorne and Nancy Henley, eds., *Language and Sex: Difference and Dominance.* Rowley, Mass.: Newbury House, 1975.

This overview of literature on the sexual differentiation of language begins with a brief history of this field of research (with emphasis on the contributions of the women's movement), and a review of the diverse disciplines, frameworks, and methods of research which have converged on this topic. Sociolinguistic distinctions—verbal repertoire, speech style, and the social context of communicative events—are used to interpret and organize various findings about sex differences in speech, and to suggest leads for further research. The bulk of the article is devoted to the issue of social context, to trying to account for the sexual differentiation of language by drawing on theories and research on the sociology, anthropology, and psychology of the sexes. There are three central themes: (1) The social elaboration of gender differences through learned, including linguistic, behavior; (2) Language and male dominance, expressed in sexist language (language about women) and, in actual speech use, in verbal gestures of dominance and submission between men and women (e.g., patterns of interruption, hesitation, amount of talk; the less obtrusive speech of women; speech genres such as asymmetric joking). The finding that female speech is more polite and "correct" is related to the greater circumspection required of subordinates and to the connection Trudgill suggests between masculinity and less standard speech forms. There is a discussion of whether men's speech is superior, drawing attention to the dangers in assuming the male as the norm, and suggesting that there is a need to reevaluate, but perhaps not discard female speech patterns. And there is analysis of under what conditions and with what consequences women and men use the speech style associated with the opposite sex; (3) The division of labor by sex—language is part of the ideological association of women with family, and men with occupational roles. There may be a sexual division of labor in conversational topics and lexicons, and male and female speech can be compared for range, extent, and locales of use. The traditional responsibility of women for child-rearing gives them a central role in transmitting language; the roles of the family and of peer groups in language acquisition, and the tie of language to single-sex bonding are discussed. Finally, the paper turns to the issue of change, and summarizes some of the many questions and topics awaiting systematic inquiry.

II. VOCABULARY AND SYNTAX

A. Sexist Bias of English Language

1. Analysis of Sexism in Language

BODINE, ANN.
"Androcentrism in Prescriptive Grammar." *Language in Society,* in press.

Although prescriptive grammarians have, at least since the 18th century, claimed that there is no sex-indefinite pronoun for the third person singular and stated that *he* is to be used, English "has always had other linguistic devices for referring to sex-indefinite referents, notably, the use of *they* (their, them)," as in the sentence: "Who dropped their ticket?" Prior to the 18th century, the singular *they* was widely used in written and presumably also spoken English. It is significant, Bodine suggests, that grammarians sought to correct it by focusing on agreement with the antecedent in number, but not in gender. "A non-sexist 'correction' would have been to advocate *he or she,* but rather than encourage this usage the grammarians actually tried to eradicate it also, claiming *he or she* is 'clumsy,' 'pedantic,' or 'unnecessary.' Significantly, they never attacked terms such as *one or more* or *person or persons,* although the plural logically includes the singular more than the masculine includes the feminine. These two situations are analogous. In both cases the language user is confronted with an obligatory category, either number or sex, which is irrelevant to the message being transmitted." Current junior high and high school grammars condemn *he or she* as clumsy, and the singular *they* as inaccurate; "and then the pupils are taught to achieve both elegance of expression and accuracy by referring to women as *he*!" Bodine cites examples she has collected from ordinary conversations of people using *they* for singular antecedents. The continuing attack of textbook writers and teachers on *he or she* and the singular *they,* she notes, also indicates "both forms are still much a part of American English." Earlier changes in second person pronouns (e.g. the elimination of *thou-thee* under egalitarian pressures) demonstrate that pronominal systems are susceptible to alteration in response to social change. Bodine predicts that the feminist counter-attack on the sex-indefinite *he* will affect English pronominal usage; "during the next few years students of language development may have the opportunity to follow the progress of a particularly visible type of language change." Such change will bear on general linguistic issues: post-childhood linguistic acculturation; conscious vs. unconscious change; and compensatory adjustment within the linguistic system (e.g. the possible weakening of number concord).

BOSMAJIAN, HAIG A.
    "The Language of Sexism." *ETC.,* 29 (1972), 305-313.

This is a general article about sexism in language, which takes off from the point that language has often been used to "define and dehumanize individuals or groups of individuals into submission" (e.g. the Nazi use of language to redefine and dehumanize the Jews; the language of white racism). Examples of "male supremist language" are given: the use of male as generic; the "firstness of *men*" when listed with *women* (an ordering that appears even in the N.O.W. 1966 Statement of Purpose, which begins "We, men and women who hereby constitute ourselves as the National Organization for Women"); the language of religions and of organizations (*spokesmen*); the ritual of women adopting the name of their husbands upon marriage, and of giving the newborn child the male parent's surname. In short, men have a power of defining through naming, and, the author argues (citing examples of such efforts), the liberation of women "will have to be accompanied with a conscious effort on the part of women to allow themselves to be defined by men no longer."

BURR, ELIZABETH, SUSAN DUNN, AND NORMA FARQUHAR.
    "Women and the Language of Inequality." *Social Education,* 36 (1972), 841-845.

A brief article which points to sexist writing customs, especially in textbooks. Examples: Subsuming masculine terms in fact operate to exclude females (a phrase like "men of goodwill" does not bring to mind a group of amicable females). In textbooks, hypothetical persons are usually male ("a discontented man could move west"). Girls and women are usually referred to mainly in terms of those who "own" them, as nameless wives, daughters, and mothers of named males. Because women have traditionally been expected to assume the full burden of childcare, textbooks describe children who still need care as the mother's ("Sacajewea carried her infant son"); male offspring seen as heirs and female offspring of marriageable age are described as the father's. Women are often described as if they were luggage ("the pioneer took his family west in a covered wagon"), which is inappropriate unless the woman moved involuntarily. Textbooks should also acknowledge the fact that single women and female heads of family participated in the westward movement. Terms which are applicable to either or both sexes are often defined as applying exclusively to males (*monarchy* = 'a nation ruled by a king').

CONNERS, KATHLEEN.
    "Studies in Feminine Agentives in Selected European Languages." *Romance Philology*, 24 (1971), 573-598.

A lengthy analysis of the history of the formation of feminine agentives, especially for occupational terms (e.g. *aviatrix*), in the major Romance languages, English, and German. Feminine agentives behave as the marked category vis-à-vis the masculine terms (which serve as the generic, and to designate mixed groups). Yet feminine agentives are no more uniform in derivation than masculine ones, a fact Conners attributes to four non-linguistic factors: (1) In most occupations the need for an explicitly feminine label arises infrequently because the masculine can represent both sexes in its unmarked generic function, and most occupations have been confined to men; (2) The feminine counterparts of masculine terms often designate the wife of the man practicing the occupation (*duchess* is the spouse of *duke*); (3) The form potentially fit to serve as a feminine agentive has often been preempted by the corresponding name of an instrument, container, or product (e.g. in French *faucheuse* means 'mowing machine'); (4) Individual feminine agentives and suffixes have repeatedly taken on derogatory or facetious connotations "regardless of whether the society involved regarded women with respect and nourished their ambitions." While many new feminine agentives are coined, sometimes experimentally, there does not seem to be spreading acceptance and use of such forms proportionate to the movement of women into the labor force, at least in Western European societies. In these societies, "as the socially marked category, women in public life, becomes gradually less marked (i.e., as women become more and more common in traditionally 'masculine' occupations), it gradually becomes less rather than more appropriate to distinguish sex morphologically." On the other hand, "in modern Russia and Israel, where for political and historical reasons women have shared greatly in the work of a society in the making, feminizers seem to enjoy great productivity, unblocked by any threat of confusion with words for machines, where skilled labor is at issue, or by any strong tendency toward facetious connotations . . . Could the high frequency of female occupational terms actually tend to lessen the possibility of their degradation to facetious use?"

DENSMORE, DANA.
    "Speech Is the Form of Thought." Reprint (10 pp.) available from KNOW, Inc., P.O. Box 86031, Pittsburgh, Pa. 15221.

Sexism is so pervasive that language reflects it, for example, in pronouns (*he* as the generic for *he* or *she,* even in a group which is 99% women). Densmore proposes a new glossary of personal pronouns: nominative case, *she* (includes in one word both the old *he* and the old *she*); objective case, *herm* (includes *her* and *him*); possessive case, *heris* (used for *her* or *his*, including both words in spelling and sound). In place of *man* as the generic, there should be more use of *human, person, people.* The author concludes: "Androcentric language is first a symptom of sexism, but it also reinforces it and permits abuses such as subtly shutting women out. To the extent that it is a symptom, enforcing these changes will not abolish sexism. But it would raise consciousness and permit women to begin to feel that they are not a different species, not, in fact, a useful afterthought lodged between man and nature."

FARB, PETER.
  Word Play: What Happens When People Talk. New York: Alfred A. Knopf, 1973.

  Written in a lively style for a general audience, this book includes several sections which summarize studies of sex differences in language. On pp. 141-144, Farb writes of "the unequal treatment many languages give to the two sexes": the use of male generics, the notion that the average person is always masculine (as in "the man in the street" and hypothetical person in riddles), the connotations of various sets of words (males *roar, bellow,* and *growl;* females *squeal, shriek,* and *purr*). While *woman* began as an "Adam's-rib word" (derived from Old English *wife* plus *man*), *female* came from the Middle English word, *femelle,* meaning 'small woman,' but due to its apparent resemblance to the word *male,* it got changed to *female.* Masculine words like *master* and *father* are usually used to refer to leadership and power; feminine words more often imply unpredictability or treachery (e.g. feminine names for hurricanes). Farb also discusses sexism in French (feminine nouns are formed by adding -*e* to the masculine; words for high-prestige roles are usually masculine). [*See II-B, III-A, III-B-2, V.*]

FARWELL, MARILYN.
  "Women and Language." In Jean R. Leppaluoto, ed., *Women on the Move.* Pittsburgh: KNOW, Inc., 1973, pp. 165-171.

  The English language, Farwell writes, "reflects and rigidifies the social status of women"; its structure "solidifies the either/or pattern of masculine and feminine and discourages an equalization pattern, one that would emphasize the person instead of the role." Structures like the generic male pronoun and nouns like *poet, actor,* and *Jew* define woman as "secondary or other, even as deviant." The connotations of various words imply that women are weak, immature, and even childish; terms like *effete* and *effeminate,* and the use of the term *masculine* to describe accented and therefore strong endings in poetry, imply that to be female is to be weak. The feminine sometimes connotes seductive and dangerous. To overcome sexist language, Farwell suggests spreading awareness of these patterns, introducing non-male generic terms and pronouns (our goal should be to make terms like *chairperson* familiar), and drawing upon the creative language of writers like Sylvia Plath and Adrienne Rich.

FAUST, JEAN.
  "Words That Oppress." *Women Speaking,* April, 1970. Reprint (2 pp.) available from KNOW, Inc., P.O. Box 86031, Pittsburgh, Pa. 15221.

  Language "oppresses and diminishes the female of the species, reducing her to an appendage or an extension of the male." Titles, professions, occupations are masculine, and are diminished when made feminine by adding -*ess* or -*ette* (*sculptress, jockette*). Male athletic teams have forceful names (*Lions, Tigers, Rams*); female teams are called names like *Rockettes, Mercurettes, Cindergals.* Language emphasizes differences between the sexes; language controls behavior and thought. Women are often defined by their sexuality (rarely are men "defined so wholly and irrevocably in a single word"), e.g. *whore, slut, tart.* Since World War II, Faust claims, sexual insults have increased. She concludes that men's fear of women, and of sexual inadequacy, is behind this derogatory language.

FEMINIST WRITERS WORKSHOP.
   (Proposed by Ruth Todasco; commentaries by Ruth Todasco, Ellen Morgan, Jessie Sheridan, and Kathryn Starr). *An Intelligent Woman's Guide to Dirty Words: English Words and Phrases Reflecting Sexist Attitudes Toward Women in Patriarchal Society, Arranged According to Usage and Idea.* Vol. One of *The Feminist English Dictionary.* Chicago: Loop Center Y.W.C.A. (37 South Wabash Ave.), 1973.

   This is the first in a series designed to review language as a prime force in the deprecation of women, to jar lexicographers to "perceive the prejudice inherent in their scholarship," and to provide a new set of definitions to substitute for those, like Webster, whose authority derives from male-dominated culture. Vol. One draws material from established dictionaries of the English language, arranging words and definitions under the categories: "Woman as Whore"; "Woman as Whorish"; "Woman as Body"; "Woman as Animal"; "Woman as -Ess"; "Woman as -Ette"; "Patriarchal Stereotypes." The commentators note that language functions to keep women in their place, that it embodies "the self-deluding myths of patriarchal man," that it deprecates, diminishes, and expresses contempt toward women, and defines them as a subspecies "different from the human standard." Ellen Morgan comments that "neo-feminists" are building consciousness of the conditioning force of language, and instituting reforms to negate the force of linguistic sexism. Neo-feminists also "try to create in their writing an affirmation of femaleness, to develop a linguistic mode which conditions positively," for example by describing female sexuality and femaleness in complimentary terms reflecting the value of "gentleness and other qualities which they believe have been concomitants of women's powerlessness and oppression." While many men use an authoritative and declarative linguistic mode, neo-feminists "tend to reject elitism and authoritarianism, and base their politics on personal experience, their style is more descriptive and, if not more tentative, more relative, more inclined to the many-faceted, less structured by the desire to assert one idea to the exclusion of others than to convey the multiple and personal character of experience."

GRAHAM, ALMA.
   "The Making of a Nonsexist Dictionary." *Ms.,* 2 (Dec., 1973), 12-16. Reprinted in Barrie Thorne and Nancy Henley, eds., *Language and Sex: Difference and Dominance.* Rowley, Mass.: Newbury House, 1975.

   An account of the construction of the *American Heritage School Dictionary* (American Heritage Publishing Co., 1972), the first ever published in which lexicographers made a conscious effort to correct the sex biases of English. The dictionary, a wordbook for children, contains 35,000 entries selected after a computer analysis of 5 million words encountered by American children in their schoolbooks. 700,000 citation slips were prepared, each showing a word in 3 lines of context. These slips gave the analysis a reflection of the culture talking to its children, and enabled them to compile statistics on sex-linked word usage in context. Some of the statistics: the ratio in schoolbooks of *he* to *she, him* to *her,* and *his* to *hers* was almost 4 to 1; there were over 7 times as many men as women in the books, and over twice as many boys as girls. *Mother* occurred more frequently than *father, wife* 3 times as often as *husband;* women are referred to in terms that identify their relation to men and children. Additionally, the citation slips showed that boys and girls were being taught separate sets of values, expectations, and goals, along expected lines: "masculine" activity, strength, etc., were contrasted with "feminine" inactivity and beauty. The lexicographers consciously combatted these images, developing new illustrative usages running counter to stereotypes. Graham also identifies some ways that sexism works in the language: (1) the "my-virtue-is-your-vice" tactic: a man's tears are *womanish*, a woman's uniform, *mannish;* (2) labelling the "exception to the rule," as in *woman doctor* and *male nurse;* (3) the "trivializing tactic," producing female forms like *poetess* and *libber;* (4) the "praise him/blame her" tendency, as in the contrast between *queen, madam, dame,* and *prince, lord, father;* (5) the "exclusionary tactic" that assumes all the world is male. Graham discusses the use of male forms to refer to human beings in general, and cites a finding from a survey of pronoun citations: out of 940 citations for *he*, 744 were applied to male humans, 128 to male animals, and 36 to persons in male-linked occupations; only 32 referred to the unspecified singular subject. Thus the reason most pronouns in schoolbooks were male was because most of the subjects being written about were males, not because the references were to unidentified human beings.

GREER, GERMAINE.
  The Female Eunuch. New York: McGraw-Hill, 1971.

  In a chapter on "Abuse," Greer discusses "the language of women hatred." She notes that some terms which originally applied to both sexes have become pejorative when applied to women (e.g. *witches* may be either sex, but as a term of abuse, the word is directed at women). Class antagonism enters into the vocabulary of female status with the ironic use of terms like *madam, lady,* and *dame.* "The most offensive group of words applied to the female population are those which bear the weight of neurotic male disgust for illicit or casual sex" (e.g., *tramp, piece of ass, pig, pussy*). Many of these terms are "dead, fleshy and inhuman." There is also food imagery (*honey, sweety-pie*), pretty toy words *(doll)*, cute animal terms *(chick)*.

HAUGEN, EINAR.
  "Sexism and the Norwegian Language." Paper presented at Society for the Advancement of Scandinavian Study meeting, 1974. (Haugen is in the Program in Scandinavian Germanic Languages and Literatures, Harvard Univ.)

  Haugen traces controversy in Scandinavia over sexism in language. The women's rights movement in Norway has called attention to language as a factor in male dominance, and the writings of Rolf M. Blakar (a social psychologist at the Univ. of Oslo) on sexism in language have "caused a bit of a stir." Blakar offers evidence from use of titles of address, descriptions of occupations, the synonyms for *man* and *woman,* word association tests, and the listing of husbands and wives in official registers. As counter-measures, Blakar proposes what amount to "consciousness-raising" techniques, e.g., reversal, such as speaking of a "male judge" or "career man" or "chatterbox men." In his conclusion, Haugen notes that "language expresses faithfully, if a little conservatively, the realities as the vast number of men and women have seen it down to our day." When the reality changes, the language will respond. [One of Blakar's writings: Rolf M. Blakar, "How Sex Roles are Represented, Reflected and Conserved in the Norwegian Language," *Olso Univ. Working Papers in Linguistics,* 5 (1974). [*See III-A.*]

KEY, MARY RITCHIE.
    "Linguistic Behavior of Male and Female." *Linguistics,* 88 (Aug. 15, 1972), 15-31.

There are different male and female images in language: men *bellow,* women *purr;* men *yell,* women *scream* or *squeal; vivacious* women, but not *vivacious* men; women *fret,* men *get angry;* men *have careers,* women *have jobs;* married women engage in *homemaking,* single women *keep house.* Key gives examples, drawn from written and spoken language, of groupings in which "women" occur, e.g., "the blind, the lame, and the women" (Nathan Pusey); signs on Mohammedan mosques: "Women and dogs and other impure animals are not permitted to enter"; it is difficult to tame "oceans, fools, and women" (Spiro Agnew); women are often classified with slaves and children. Key discusses pronominal referents; although grammar books may say the stated pronoun *he* is used in reference to an unspecified, unknown person, in actual usages certain occupational roles may be referred to as *she* (nurses; elementary school teachers; secretaries), in contrast with the invariable *he* with doctor; sailor; plumber; president. Pronominal and nominal referents are often inconsistent. [*See I, II-B, III-B-3.*]

LAKOFF, ROBIN.
    "Language and Woman's Place." *Language in Society,* 2 (1973), 45-79.

Lakoff explores ways in which language refers to women, as distinct from men: (1) There are more euphemisms for "woman" than for "man" (e.g., *lady; girl*). Euphemisms indicate the subject is a source of strain or discomfort; there are often derogatory epithets for which the euphemism substitutes. To banish *lady* in its euphemistic sense, we would need first to get rid of *broad* and other derogatory terms for women (and the idea that women *are* broads). The euphemisms may themselves be degrading, e.g. *lady* tends to trivialize the subject matter *(lady doctor); girl* in stressing the idea of immaturity, removes the sexual connotations lurking in *woman,* but also suggests irresponsibility. (2) Language forms which define women as secondary beings who achieve status only through men, e.g., supposedly parallel words, which in fact are imbalanced (and indicate social inequities): *master* and *mistress* have diverged in time; *master* now refers to a man who has acquired consummate ability in some field, while *mistress* is restricted to its sexual sense of 'paramour' (and, unlike *master,* is preceded by a possessive masculine noun: not "she is a mistress," but "she is John's mistress"). Analogously, we say "Mary is John's widow," but not "John is Mary's widower" (though he is dead, she is still defined by her relationship to him, but the bereaved husband is no longer defined in terms of his wife). There is a lack of parallel in terms of address for each sex: *Mr.* (ambiguous re marital status) vs. *Mrs./Miss.* There is a tendency to use first names sooner and to be more apt to use them (rather than last-name-alone, or title-plus-last-name) in referring to and addressing women. In terms of changes, Lakoff argues that language is a clue to social inequities, which must be changed before language will change. She maintains that there is currently too much emphasis on neutralizing pronouns (removing the generic *he*), an area which is less in need of changing than other areas of linguistic sexism, and which is more difficult to change than many other disparities. [*See I, II-B, III-B-3, V, VII.*]

LAWRENCE, BARBARA.
    "Dirty Words *Can* Harm you." *Redbook,* 143 (May, 1974), 33.

An essay which points to the systematic derogation of women implicit in many obscenities. Various tabooed sexual verbs (e.g. *fuck; screw*) involve origins and imagery with "undeniably painful, if not sadistic, implications, the object of which is almost always female." When not openly deprecating to women, tabooed male descriptions may serve to "divorce a male organ or function from any significant interaction with the female" (e.g., *testes,* suggesting "witnesses" to the sexual and procreative strengths of the male organ). Female descriptives, on the other hand, are usually contemptuous of women (e.g. *piece*). Lawrence notes that many people who are shocked at racial or ethnic obscenities do not question obscenities which derogate women.

LEGMAN, G.
    Rationale of the Dirty Joke: An Analysis of Sexual Humor. Castle Books, 1968.

This study analyzes over 2000 erotic jokes and folklore collected in America and abroad. It is arranged by subjects (such as "the male approach," "the sadistic concept," and "women"), with extensive tangents, e.g. into the significance of jokes about mothers-in-law and about pubic hair. Legman claims that most "dirty jokes" are originated by men and there is no place in such folklore for women, except as the butt of humor. "It is not just that so preponderant an amount of the material is grossly anti-woman in tendency and intent, but also that the situations presented almost completely lack any protagonist position in which a woman can identify herself—*as a woman*—with any human gratification or pride." Legman argues that speech is a form of sexual display for males, akin to bodily ornamentation for females. [*See III-B-4; IV-C.*]

MAINARDI, PATRICIA.
    "Quilts: The Great American Art." *Radical America,* 7, No. 1 (1973), 36-68.

In this article on quilting as women's unrecognized art, Mainardi shows the sexism implicit in much writing on quilts. For example, in his catalogue essays for recent exhibitions of quilts by the Whitney and Smithsonian museums, "Jonathan Holstein praises pieced quilts [which bear superficial resemblance to the work of contemporary formalist artists such as Stella, Noland, and Newman] with the words 'strong,' 'bold,' 'vigorous,' 'bravado,' and 'toughness,' while he dismisses the appliqué quilts [which current male artists have not chosen to imitate] as 'pretty,' 'elegant,' 'beautiful but decorative.' This is the kind of phallic criticism women artists are sick of hearing, and is made all the more ridiculous by the fact that women actually made *both* types of quilts" (p. 64). In a footnote, Mainardi adds, " . . . from my experience in researching this article [I found that] sentence structure can be sexist—as in the constant use of the passive voice in reference to quilts ('quilts were made,' 'quilting was done,' 'names changed,' never 'women made quilts,' 'women changed the names'), and the subtle sexism in the constant use of the word 'pattern' instead of 'design' " (p. 68).

MILLER, CASEY AND KATE SWIFT.
    "De-sexing the English Language." *Ms.,* 1 (Spring, 1972), 7.

The generic personal pronoun (*he*) has an effect on personality development, implying that women are a human subspecies, whereas it bolsters male egos. In response to women's liberation, people are "trying to kick the habit of using *he* when they mean anyone, male or female"; politicians are more careful, and *his/her* is appearing in print. Adding the feminine to the masculine pronoun is often awkward, as are other devices, such as *they* used as a singular pronoun. There is need for a new singular personal pronoun that is truly generic. The authors suggest: nominative case, *tey* (to replace *he and she*); objective case, *tem* (for *him and her*); possessive case, *ter(s)* (in place of *his and her[s]*). Once *tey* or a similar word is adopted, *he* can become exclusively masculine, just as *she* is now exclusively feminine.

MILLER, CASEY AND KATE SWIFT.
    "One Small Step for Genkind." *New York Times Magazine,* April 16, 1972, pp. 36+.
    Reprinted as "Is Language Sexist?" *Cosmopolitan,* Sept., 1972, pp. 89-92+.

Sexist language is "any language that expresses stereotyped attitudes and expectations or assumes the inherent superiority of one sex over the other." *Masculine* and *feminine* are more sexist than *male* and *female,* because the words invoke strong cultural stereotypes. Words associated with males (*manly, virile, masculine*) often imply positive traits like courage, strength, independence; corresponding words associated with females are defined with fewer attributes (weakness is often one of them), and are often used in a negative way (*feminine wiles; womanish tears*). *Sissy,* derived from *sister,* is pejorative; *buddy,* from *brother,* is positive. The media use language in a sexist way: when a woman or girl makes the news, her sex is identified at the beginning of a story, if possible in the headline (which reveals an assumption that woman's achieving is rare). Because people are assumed to be male unless otherwise identified, the media have developed an extensive vocabulary to avoid repetition of *woman.* The results ("Grandmother Wins Nobel Prize"; "Blonde Hijacks Airliner") convey information that would be ludicrous if the subjects were male. The addition of feminine endings to non-sexual words (*poetess; aviatrix*) declined before the start of the new feminist movement, but there is now a kind of counter-movement, e.g. for *chairwoman; congresswoman.*

MURRAY, JESSICA.
    "Male Perspective in Language." *Women: A Journal of Liberation,* 3, No. 2 (1973), 46-50.

Language reflects "the archetypical assumption" that "all people are male until proven female." For example, the supposedly generic and neutral meaning of *man* is often confused with the male meaning; a lecture beginning with a general philosophical question, "How does Man see himself?", continued "As a salesman? A doctor? A dentist?" Hence the scope was shifted from man, the species, to man, to male. Was Eve the vehicle of man (the male)'s Fall or of man (the species)'s Fall? This involves a paradox: women being part of humanity, but conceptually excluded from it. Murray offers other examples from art, literature, and textbooks showing that people are assumed to be male unless specified female. A conspicuous example of woman-as-special-case is the sexualization of women, the assumption in language, writing, and the media, that a woman's gender is the most significant thing about her (while men are considered full people, whose sexuality is only a small part of their whole make-up). Murray concludes, "the role of language in perpetuating the archetype of women-as-extra-human could be changed by adopting new language conventions" (e.g. *Ms.*, and changes in the pronoun system), but "let us not do away with male-initiated terminology until we fully understand from whence it came."

NICHOLS, PATRICIA C.
"The Uses of Gender in English." Unpublished (graduate student) paper (12 pp.), Committee on Linguistics, Stanford Univ.

Nichols argues (as does Lakoff) that since pronouns are so integral to language, it would be difficult to introduce a new, non-sexist set of gender pronouns into English. But "there exist now within the language other means by which to change the uses of gender which relegate women to an invisible or inferior status." Increasingly, people are experimenting with gender usage: *he or she* is increasingly used generically; in informal usage, many speakers select a plural pronoun to refer to an indefinite pronoun or noun of unknown sex ("If a person were in trouble, they could have someplace to go"). There are deviations, especially in informal language, from the convention that masculine is the unmarked or norm, and feminine, the marked or deviation from the norm, e.g. the chairman of a grocery store in a television interview: "The consumer is entitled to all of the information she wants" (reflecting a view that women are the consumers). Nichols suggests more systematic study of uses of gender in everyday language, and research on children's acquisition of the generic *he* (is it part of casual language or more a feature of school language?)

NILSEN, ALLEEN PACE.
"The Correlation Between Gender and Other Semantic Features in American English." Paper presented at Linguistic Society of America meetings, Dec., 1973.

Nilsen found 500 dictionary items which included either a visible marker of +Masculine (e.g., *fellow, son, man*) or of +Feminine (e.g., *daughter, girl, frau*), the gender markers achieved through derivation rather than coincidence. These terms were analyzed for the existence of certain semantic features, and the results compared with the masculine/ feminine markers, with the following results noted: There were 385 masculine terms and only 132 feminine ones, a ratio of roughly 3:1. This ratio was approximated in the category of archaic or rare words, but with all other areas the ratio differed considerably. Among words marked for +Person in the generic sense, all 90 were +Masculine. Among words marked +Occupation, the ratio of masculine to feminine words is almost 5:1 (and a larger proportion of the masculine than of feminine ones are also archaic/rare). For words marked +Prestige, there were 108 masculine and 18 feminine words (about 6:1, double the overall ratio). In words marked for +Negative connotation, feminine words outnumbered masculine ones 25 to 20 (and many are occupation-related). Among words marked −Human (no longer referring to a person although the lexical base originally did, such as *lady slipper, king pin*) 82 were masculine and 35 feminine. Words marked +Abstract are similar to the −Human, but they are also −Concrete; the ratio of masculine to feminine words was about 2:1 (43 to 21). The feminine words for these two categories (−Human, +Abstract) "tended to deal with aesthetically pleasing little things," e.g., *lady bird, maidenhair fern;* the masculine words were more serious, e.g., *mastermind, fraternalism.* For words marked +Unusual age, there were 34 feminine and 27 masculine terms, supporting the idea that age is more relevant to women than to men in our culture. Nearly all the age terms have positive connotations, incorporating the concept of youth, but there were five negative-connotation terms denoting old females, and none for old males. Among words marked for +Family relationship feminine terms most outnumbered masculine ones, 46:32. There was a correlation between the generic and prestige terms (both highly masculine). For some of the generic terms, specifically feminine terms have been created, but this doesn't guarantee linguistic equality; for example, the masculine term travels into other lexical items, as in *king-queen-kingdom* (but not *queendom*). There is another group of words in which the basic word is not gender-marked, but a feminine word has been derived, e.g., *author-authoress* and *major-majorette* (the latter having a different meaning). Apparently the *-er/-or* suffix, meaning "doer," has acquired a male connotation. It also seems that "the higher the prestige . . . of the word, the more important it becomes to make a separation between males and females." Nilsen raises several questions relating to feminists' desires to attack linguistic sexism, and concludes that feminists might best concentrate efforts on "educating children and the general public to the way language is rather than by trying to change the language," particularly seeing that, for instance, when generic male terms are used, illustrations of both males and females are given.

NILSEN, ALLEEN PACE.
   "Sexism in English: A Feminist View." In Nancy Hoffman, Cynthia Secor, and Adrian Tinsley, eds., *Female Studies VI.* Old Westbury, N.Y.: The Feminist Press, 1972, pp. 102-109.

   Culling through a standard desk dictionary, Nilsen found a variety of examples of sexism in English, which fit into three patterns: (1) "In our culture it is a woman's body which is considered important while it is a man's mind or his activities which are valued. A woman is sexy. A man is successful." Far more words have been derived from male names (e.g. *pasteurization, sousaphone, shick test*) than from female names (the only two in common use, *bloomers* and *Mae West jacket*, are both related to woman's physical anatomy). In geographical names, there is a preoccupation with women's breasts (*The Tetons, Little Nipple Top, Maiden's Peak*), but not with male anatomy (*Jackson Hole, Pike's Peak*). In words with a male and female counterpart, the female word often has sexual connotations, while the male word retains "a serious business-like aura," e.g. *sir* vs. *madam; master* vs. *mistress.* In other pairs of words, the masculine is usually the base with a feminine suffix added (e.g. *hero* and *heroine*); the masculine word "travels into compounds while the feminine word is a dead end" (e.g. *kingdom* but not *queendom*). Sex and marriage is the only semantic area "in which the masculine word is not the base or more powerful word," e.g. *prostitute* is the base word, and *male prostitute,* the derivative; *bridegroom* is derived from *bride,* and *widower* from *widow.* (2) Language indicates that women are expected to play a passive role, and men an active one, e.g. the frequent identification of women with something to eat (*a peach*), with plants (*wall flower*), the passivity of many female names

(Ivy, Pearl). Females are also identified with pets *(pony tails;* dressed in *halters).* Another aspect of women's passivity: their definition in relationship to husbands, brothers, and fathers. (3) In language, the concept of masculine usually has positive connotations, while the feminine has either trivial or negative connotations (compare *chef* with *cook; tailor* with *seamstress; major* with *majorette).* Telling a child to *be a lady* often means to sit with her knees together; *to be a man* means to be noble, strong, virtuous. "The chicken metaphor tells the whole story of a girl's life. In her youth she is a *chick,* then she marries and begins feeling *cooped up,* so she goes to *hen parties* where she *cackles* with her friends. Then she has her *brood* and begins to *hen-peck* her husband. Finally she turns into an *old biddy.*"

SCHNEIDER, JOSEPH W. AND SALLY L. HACKER.
   "Sex Role Imagery and the Use of the Generic 'Man' in Introductory Texts."
   American Sociologist, 8, No. 8 (1973), 12-18.

Students in introductory sociology classes were asked to submit pictures to represent the major sections of an introductory text. When the terms used the generic *man (social man, political man, economic man, urban man),* 64% of the pictures showed male only. When the generic label *man* was removed (so the terms were *social behavior, political behavior,* etc.), 50% of the students illustrated the concepts with pictures of males' only. Women were seldom elicited as the image under the generic term *man.*

SCHULZ, MURIEL R.
   "The Semantic Derogation of Woman." In Barrie Thorne and Nancy Henley, eds.,
   Language and Sex: Difference and Dominance. Rowley, Mass.: Newbury House,
   1975.

This is a study of the tendency for terms designating women in English to acquire debased or obscene reference (pejoration), and an analysis of the reasons for it, since language reflects the thoughts, attitudes, and culture of its creators and users, who in the case of English are, according to Schulz, "largely men." Schulz examines a collection of terms which have been thus abased, comparing them often with their male equivalents; terms for males have almost totally escaped such pejoration. A common tendency of the terms applied to women has been for them to become sexually abusive, i.e., to finally acquire the meaning of morally loose, whore. Women have not coined the terms; it is men who refer to women in sexual terms, and the wealth of terms reveals their hostility. Endearments for women (but not for men) have similarly undergone pejoration; a number of the terms began as references to either sex, but specialized to refer to women at the time they began pejorating. Ullman has suggested three origins for pejoration, which might bear on the causes for the degeneration of terms designating women: association with a contaminating concept, euphemism, and prejudice. Contamination may be a factor, but Schulz rejects the notion "that there is a quality inherent in the concept of *woman* which taints any word associated with it." Women are acknowledged as the *less* promiscuous, more proper, of the sexes, yet have the largest category of words designating humans in sexual terms (Schulz knows about 1000, and cites other sources). Euphemism seems out; though many terms for prostitutes are euphemistic, most are dysphemistic. Prejudice seems the most likely explanation—"woman" is a "label of primary potency"(Allport) by which a stereotype is maintained, and evidence is brought forward for fear of women as the source of the prejudice. Schulz concludes that though we generally cannot know the extent to which language influences its users, words "highly charged with emotion, taboo, or distaste do not only reflect the culture which uses them. They teach and perpetuate the attitudes which created them . . . to brand a class of person as obscene is to taint them to the users of the language."

STANLEY, JULIA P.
   "Paradigmatic Woman: The Prostitute." Paper presented, in briefer versions, at South Atlantic Modern Language Assoc., 1972; American Dialect Society, 1972; and Linguistic Society of America, 1973.

Stanley has compiled and analyzed 220 terms for sexually promiscuous women (she stopped at that number because she'd "reached the point of diminishing returns"; she notes "the very size of the set and the impossibility of collecting ALL the terms for prostitute is a comment on our culture. As linguists we assume that the existence of a new lexical item indicates a cultural need for a term that expresses a new concept. Isn't it strange that the set of terms that refer to prostitutes is one that's constantly expanding?") In contrast, there are relatively few terms for promiscuous men; Stanley lists 22, and notes "there's no linguistic reason why the set is so small." Stanley sets out the semantic features that define the categories represented by the terms for prostitutes: A. Denotative: 1. cost (cheap; expensive); 2. method of payment (direct, indirect); 3. type of activity (little; much); and Connotative: 1. negative; 2. neutral; 3. positive. B. Dysphemistic or euphemistic (whether the term exposes male disdain for the sexuality of women or conceals his disdain). C. Metonymic (whether the term refers to women through reference to a specific portion of their bodies). D. Metaphoric (whether the term refers to women through comparison to another object or animal). This semantic set provides "a paradigm of the definition of women in our culture." "The names that men have given to women who make themselves sexually available to them reveal the underlying metaphors by which men conceive of their relationships with women, and through which women learn to perceive and define themselves. The metaphors that underlie the terms for sexually promiscuous women define and perpetuate the ambivalent sex-role stereotypes that a male-dominated culture sets forth for women."

STRAINCHAMPS, ETHEL.
   "Our Sexist Language." In Vivian Gornick and Barbara K. Moran, eds., *Woman in Sexist Society*. New York: Basic Books, 1971, pp. 240-250.

An article with a philological bent, tracing the historical origins, use, and censorship of *fuck, cunt, twot, condom, diaphragm* (the author claims that women, compared with men, have a "sane and rational attitude toward taboo words"). Strainchamps cites evidence of male dominance in English: *man* and *he* as generics; words which were nonemotive when they referred to either gender have become contemptuous after being applied to women alone, and some that were pejorative lost that sense when they acquired an exclusively male reference (*shrewd-shrewish* illustrate both trends). Strainchamps claims that English "retains more vestiges of the archaic sexual attitudes than any other civilized tongue."

TOTH, EMILY.
"The Politics of Linguistic Sexism." Paper presented at Modern Language Assoc., 1971. (Toth is at the Humanities Center, Johns Hopkins.)

Language shows that men have power and superiority, whereas women are defined as Other, often as passive, inferior, or invisible. Male terms are used as the unmarked forms (*man, mankind, one-man show*), with women subsumed in the male generic. Occupations, professions, careers are male (including *bachelor's* and *Master's* degrees, and *fellowships*). When a woman enters the "man's world," this is marked by a peculiar vocabulary (*female judge, madam chairman*). Abstractions, to be revealed or controlled by men, are often personified as female (science, liberty, victory, fortune). Machines or other items run or manned by men are often called *she* (ships, cars, ejaculations like "fill 'er up!" and "Thar she blows!"). Expressions for which there is no opposite-sex equivalent indicate power relationships: *brotherly love* (whereas *sisterly love* implies lesbianism); a man can be *cocksure,* but the most a woman can do is make a man feel *hen-pecked;* a man cannot be a *shrew, fishwife, virago,* or *bitch.* There are no female equivalents for *effeminate* or *emasculated.* Women's terms are often associated with littleness, confinement, cuteness (e.g. *women's liberation* abbreviated to *lib* and *libbers,* in contrast with Black Liberation and the National Liberation Front); also the *little woman,* and the *little black dress.*

VARDA ONE.
"Manglish." Reprint (4 pp.) available from KNOW, Inc., P.O. Box 86031, Pittsburgh, Pa. 15221. (Copyright by Everywoman Pub. Co., Venice, Calif., 1971.)

This paper compiles some of the material from Varda One's "Manglish" columns in the feminist newspaper, *Everywoman.* "Manglish" is the "process of the degradation of women in language," and operates by various mechanisms: (1) "The myth of lexicographic objectivity" (dictionaries, like the Bible, are treated as absolutes, yet are full of prejudice: more space is given for male items, sex-stereotyped examples are used in illustrative sentences, the masculine is presented first in a sequence where the feminine is also present, more insulting terms are included for women than men, prejudiced comments are included, and there are more drawings of men and male animals). (2) "The appendage complex" (it is assumed that men are humans and women an afterthought, e.g. in the use of the male form for both sexes, and the use of the male form as neuter, with feminine qualifiers added). (3) "Relating function to gender, usually reserving low prestige jobs for women" (the incorporation of a gender suffix in words like *policeman* and *policewoman,* and the assumption of one sex even without an explicit indicator, e.g. *tycoon* and *secretary*). (4) "Devolutionary process of words involving women" (the degeneration of previously neutral terms like *harlot* and *wench*). (5) "The subsuming of identity" (in patronymics, married names, first names, and historical omissions [words based on names of people tend to immortalize men, but not women]). (6) "The woman as 'the other' " (men postulate women as "a goal outside themselves to be mastered and conquered," e.g. anything overwhelming in nature is feminine, such as *Mother Earth, Hurricane Ida,* and the *sea,* as is anything difficult or big, such as *ships, mines, dams*). (7) "The double standard of titles" *(Miss/Mrs.* vs. *Mr.).* (8) "The use of compliments and insults." (9) "Slang expressions for sexual organs." (10) "Sexist maxims" (e.g., "women hate to work for other women"). (11) "The use of double-think" (a woman who is aggressive is called *pushy;* a man, a *go-getter*). (12) "Sexist expressions" ("we call the deadliest insect a *black widow spider,* the cruelest torture instrument an *iron maiden,* a carnivorous plant is a *Venus flytrap,* and the device for hauling prisoners is a *black Maria*").

2. Protest Against Sexist Language

Political protest is implicit in many of the writings on sexism in language, and proposals for change (e.g., for changing pronoun structures and introducing new terms like Ms., chairperson, chairone, herstory, humankind). *This movement for language change—and the conflict and controversies which have developed in its wake—is a phenomenon in itself worthy of study, as suggested in the following references.*

CONKLIN, NANCY FAIRES.
   "Perspectives on the Dialects of Women." Paper presented at American Dialect Society, 1973. (Conklin is in the Linguistics Dept., Univ. of Mich.)

   Popular and feminist literature show growing interest in women's dialects, and a questioning of linguistic convention (e.g., the introduction of *Ms.* as a term of address; criticisms of the pronoun system). Ratification of the Equal Rights Amendment may have linguistic ramifications; federal forms, such as employment forms, which currently read, "Do not mention the race, religion, or national origin of the applicant," may have to add "sex of applicant." "It will be extremely difficult to avoid some sex-marking item such as title or third person pronoun. Perhaps some language planning is in order." Younger women, and feminist women of all ages, have begun to punctuate their speech with what have been male epithets and, in general, to avoid extremely polite styles. This change in speech may be an important predictive variable for research on the political and social attitudes of the young, middle-class, particularly college women. [*See IV-B, V.*]

CONKLIN, NANCY FAIRES.
   "Toward a Feminist Analysis of Linguistic Behavior." *The University of Michigan Papers in Women's Studies*, 1, No. 1 (1974), 51-73.

   The women's movement has made some attempts to deal with sexism in language, but has "unfortunately focused primarily on rather marginal problems," e.g. false etymologies like *herstory* (to replace *history*) and *himacane* (to replace *hurricane*). The third-person singular pronoun is significant as the only obligatorily sex-marked category in English, but the outlook for new, artificial forms (such as *te* or *co* for *he and she*) coming into general use is very poor, since historically pronoun systems are resistant to outside influence. *They* has strong colloquial usage as the third-person singular pronoun, and feminists should encourage the acceptability of *they*. The new title *Ms.* still embodies a sex marker (although eliminating mention of marital status); a "thorough-going program of de-sexing the language" would require replacing the *Ms.* and *Mr.* address forms by a neutral form, such as *M*. The most serious problems appear in the sexist use of language (e.g. the special connotations of the language for talking about women). One of the marks of the feminist in American society is the everyday use of the four letter epithets (*shit, fuck*, etc.) which have traditionally been taboo for women. "Obscene language is used to add emphasis to one's speech, to call attention to one's statements, and stress one's commitment to them. Feminists should be aware that they are using obscenities not just for their shock value, but because they are 'strong language' in the most literal sense of the word." [*See I, II-B, IV-C, V, VI.*]

DALY, MARY.
> *Beyond God the Father: Toward a Philosophy of Women's Liberation.* Boston:
> Beacon, 1973.

One of the premises of this insightful argument for feminism is that "the symbolic and linguistic instruments for communication—which include essentially the whole theological tradition in world religions—have been formulated by males under the conditions of patriarchy." Women have had the power of naming stolen from them. "We have not been free to use our own power to name ourselves, the world, or God." Part of liberation is discovering the inadequacy of existing language, and establishing a new reality by creating new words and meanings; for example, "the word *sisterhood* no longer means a subordinate mini-brotherhood, but an authentic bonding of women on a wide scale for our own liberation." Daly refers to the "gift of tongues" as an example of "the failure of religious charisma to uproot alienative structures," since speaking in tongues "has functioned as only a temporary release for individuals in elite groups," and these same individuals and groups "have been most stubbornly conservative and sexist in their adherence to 'real' language, outside the special moments of charismatic occurrences." "Women's new hearing and naming is cosmic upheaval, in contrast to this charism which is a controllable and cooptable ripple of protest. Feminist naming is a deliberate confrontation with language structures of our heritage. It transcends the split between nonrational sounds of 'tongues' and the merely rational semantic games of linguistic analysis, for it is a break out of the deafening noise of sexist language that has kept us from hearing our own word."

EBLE, CONNIE.
> "How to Name a Revolution." Paper presented at Southeastern Conference on
> Linguistics, 1973. (Eble is in the English Dept., Univ. of North Carolina.)

With the development of the women's liberation movement, "the problem that has no name" (as Betty Friedan referred to the female plight in 1966) has acquired many names. Eble divides the "working vocabulary" of the movement into four subject areas: (1) "The vocabulary of male supremacy" (e.g. *patriarchy, sexism, male chauvinist, male heavies*); (2) "The vocabulary of female unity" (e.g. *sisters, sisterhood, uppity women*); (3) "The vocabulary of action-reform-revolution" (e.g. *politics of experience, psychology of oppression, consciousness-raising*); (4) "The vocabulary of shock" (deliberate use of hostile and obscene terms to overcome stereotypes of feminine language). The media have also coined terms, many of them designed to trivialize the movement (e.g. *women's lib, lib lady, libber, libbie, bra-burners*).

HOLE, JUDITH AND ELLEN LEVINE.
> *Rebirth of Feminism.* New York: Quadrangle Books, 1971.

The first overall history of the new wave of feminism includes a section on "The Politics of Language," which describes language as one of the institutions feminists are questioning and seeking to change. The authors also note that the feminist movement has developed its own special language and set of symbols, e.g. *sexism, male chauvinist, sexist.*

McDOWELL, MARGARET B.
"The New Rhetoric of Woman Power." *The Midwest Quarterly*, 12 (1971), 187-198.

McDowell raises general questions, e.g., what types of rhetoric (of speakers, writers, aims, methods, and tone) can be found in the women's liberation movement? What kinds of writing and speeches oppose the movement? "What rhetorical stance on the woman question do contemporary advertising, television, and educaters assume?" How do various magazines react to the movement? How does the rhetoric of the women's movement compare with that of other protest movements, such as the New Left, black power, and 19th century feminism? The author categorizes branches of the women's movement, from radicals to members of government commissions on the status of women, and comments upon their varied rhetorics. The radical women's movement uses terms common to New Left protest of the 1960's, e.g., nouns or verbs become adjectives (*life* styles; *movement* women); extreme words replace moderate ones (*impoverished, dehumanized* vs. *discontent, frustration*); in spite of their anti-war stance, movement women have a militarist vocabulary (*struggle, power, solidarity, organize, attack, liberate*); guerilla theater groups use obscenity. Males in audiences often laugh at feminist speakers, as they did at abolitionists and suffragists in earlier times. [*This article is sometimes misinformed; its rhetorical stance, especially towards the radical movement, is mildly negative.*]

PEI, MARIO.
"The Paeon of the Liberated Woman," Chapter 6 of *Double-Speak in America*. New York: Hawthorn Books, 1973.

Writing in a chatty and critical vein about newly-minted phrases in the American public language scene, Pei catalogues various terms brought into parlance by the women's liberation movement, e.g. *sexism, sexist, male chauvinist pig, sex object, chairperson*. He notes feminist protest against media phrases like *Women's Lib Gals* and against the masculine generic pronoun structure. He also mentions satiric responses to feminist proposals for language change, such as Russell Baker's column in the *New York Times,* proposing male terms parallel to *Mrs.* and *Miss,* namely *Murm* abbreviated to *Mrm.* for a married man, and *Smur* or *Smr.* for a bachelor.

SAFILIOS-ROTHSCHILD, CONSTANTINA.
Women and Social Policy. Englewood Cliffs, N.J.: Prentice-Hall, 1974.

This book sets out to "delineate the entire map of strategies, social action, policies, and laws necessary to effectively eradicate sexism from all aspects of our lives and from the entire society" (p. viii). Under the section on "Social Policy to 'Liberate' Language" (pp. 122-126), the author mentions the effect of sexist language on the socialization of children into gender stereotypes, and on the expression and formulation of ideas. She proposes that writers should start writing high quality short stories and novels which are free of sex stereotypes; that historians and scientists should assess "established truths" to look for sexist biases; that "all the different types of explicit and implicit forms of sexism in the language must be detected, uncovered, and widely publicized and ridiculed." Passage of a legislative act could make it legal to sue mass media or leading figures or experts for using sexist rhetoric or expressions or carrying sexist features. "The gradual disappearance of sexist references, expressions, and connotations from our everyday language would have a very important effect upon women's self-concepts and degree of self-esteem, as well as upon the degree of esteem for and the type of image men have of women" (p. 126).

B. Sex Differences in Word Choice, Syntactic Usage, and Language Style

BARRON, NANCY.
>   "Sex-Typed Language: The Production of Grammatical Cases." *Acta Sociologica*, 14, No. 1-2 (1971), 24-72.

An analysis of the use of grammatical case as it varies by sex. Assuming that non-linguistic, sex-typed behavior would show up in language use, Barron drew on studies by Maccoby and others which suggest that in cognitive style, men are more analytic and women more synthetic; and that in interaction style, men are more self-oriented and women more other-oriented. From this, Barron hypothesized that "the speech of men is characterized by action and the projection of themselves as actors upon their environment; women are concerned with internal states and behaviors which would integrate other persons with themselves into the social situation." Recorded samples of teachers and pupils engaged in regular classroom activities were reconstructed (by adding implicit information deleted by grammatical or situational reduction rules), and each nominal phrase was coded for case, and by gender of speaker. It was found that the choice of case (which gives the meanings and uses of nouns in sentences) was sex-typed. Women, compared with men, produced a greater proportion of explicit participative cases (nouns with psychological state verbs, e.g. *hear, think, love*) and purposive cases (specifying the function or rationale of a person's actions). This, Barron claims, is because women are more concerned with internal psychological states and with the functions of objects for interpersonal use. Men made more use of instrumental and source cases (showing more involvement with implementation of action by means of objects), and objective cases (verbally emphasizing things, and particularly things acted upon). No sex differences were found in the use of agentive and locative cases.

BERNARDEZ-BONESATTI, TERESA.
>   "Feminist and Non-Feminist Out-Patients Compared." Paper presented at American Psychiatric Association, 1974. (Bernardez-Bonesatti is in the Dept. of Psychiatry, College of Human Medicine, Michigan State Univ.)

The author writes from her experience as a psychiatrist whose clinical practice in the last four years has included 32 non-feminist women and 28 feminists, ranging in ages from 18 to 45, of varied racial, educational, and marital backgrounds. These observations are based on the first two or three interviews with these patients. Non-feminists—who presented their problems as signs of personal inadequacy, and were compliant, submissive, and unassertive in the therapeutic context—tended to speak using passive self-references, defining the self via others, and rarely using the personal pronoun *I*. The feminists, all of whom had had experience in consciousness-raising groups, were less submissive and compliant, and more active, inquisitive, and critical towards the therapist. They were more autonomous in self-definition than the non-feminists, and used more active self-references. The author concludes that "feminists are healthier persons although they are outside the [biased] 'norm' for female behavior."

BODINE, ANN.
    "Sex Differentiation in Language." Paper presented at Conference on Women and Language, Rutgers Univ., 1973 [*this part of paper not included in revised version cited in I*].

In an informal study, Bodine found that along the East Coast men say *half dollar* for the coin that American women call *fifty cent piece* (although the introduction of the *Kennedy half dollar* has broken down that pattern). There is sex differentiation in first names and in most common titles in English. One sixth of personal nouns are sex differentiated; of those, 20% refer to religious and court hierarchy (abbess, countess), and hence are low in usage; another 20% are high usage kinship terms. Bodine discusses the origin of *man* as a generic term, and the historical and current controversy over the use of *they* with a sex-indefinite singular antecedent.

CONKLIN, NANCY FAIRES.
    "Toward a Feminist Analysis of Linguistic Behavior." *The University of Michigan Papers in Women's Studies,* 1, No. 1 (1974), 51-73.

The sexes have different word domains: women are more likely to control the terminology of sewing and fabric terms, cooking methods and utensils, and child care; men, the jargon of sports and of auto mechanics. This specialization reflects the roles and functions of each sex in society. "Since men may be professionals in any field, it is quite conceivable that men who command the vocabulary of what are generally women's subjects may be taken for professional (rather than 'amateur,' like the housewives) practitioners of that subject matter area (i.e., chefs, child psychologists, designers). Because women are more rarely professionals of any sort and almost never achieve professional status in areas which are viewed as 'male,' they are less likely to be given the benefit of the doubt (i.e., assumed to be trained mechanics, sportscasters, or even chemists, lawyers, or film directors, the 'neutral' areas)." [*See I, II-A-2, IV-C, V, VI.*]

EBLE, CONNIE C.
    "How the Speech of Some Is More Equal Than Others." Paper presented at Southeastern Conference on Linguistics, 1972. (Eble is in the English Dept., Univ. of North Carolina.)

There are sex differences in the frequency and context of use of certain words, e.g. endearment terms *(sweetie, honey, dear)* have more limited use by men; while both sexes can say, "Hi *love*," to members of the opposite sex, in America only women can say it to the same sex (in England men can say it to them). Females can use both *my boyfriend* and *my girlfriend* in relation to themselves, but men can use only *my girlfriend* in this way. In contrast, terms of hostility are more associated with men. There are sex differences in choice of adjectives, and possibly in the connotation of words. Some phrases have different meanings if spoken by a male vs. a female, e.g., "You caught me with my pants down" is a "metaphorical admission of embarrassment on the part of a man but is almost always interpreted literally and physically if a woman says it." The phrase, "he's got great legs" suggests active athletic stamina; "she's got great legs" implies a passive sexual quality. [*See III-B-3.*]

FARB, PETER.
Word Play: What Happens When People Talk. New York: Alfred A. Knopf, 1973.

This summary of sociolinguistic literature, designed for a general audience, includes a discussion of sex differences in speech use. On p. 49, Farb writes that words like *goodness, gracious,* and *dear me* are usually considered female speech. Women's speech is also associated with the expressive use of intensifiers like *so, such,* and *vastly* (a female usage which has also been observed in German, Danish, French, and Russian). [*See II-A, III-A, III-B-2, V.*]

GARCIA-ZAMOR, MARIE A.
    "Child Awareness of Sex Role Distinctions in Language Use." Paper presented at Linguistic Society of America, Dec., 1973. (Garcia-Zamor is with the International Bank for Reconstruction and Development, 1818 H St., N.W., Washington, D.C. 20433.)

Garcia-Zamor tested eight nursery school children for their tendency to *attribute* certain expressions to males or females. Boys were more in agreement over their attributions, particularly in attributing statements to males. Aggressive expressions, bright colors, cars, *shit,* and *daddy* were seen as male. *Dum dum* (associated with breaking something), light colors, tag questions, and *drat* were associated with females. [*See VII.*]

GILLEY, HOYT MELVYN AND COLLIER STEPHEN SUMMERS.
    "Sex Differences in the Use of Hostile Verbs." *Journal of Psychology,* 76 (1970), 33-37.

In this experimental study 50 males and 50 females were asked to make up sentences from a given pronoun and a given verb. There were 20 "neutral" and 20 "hostile" verbs; subjects were in either a personal-reference condition for the pronouns (*I* or *we*) or an other-reference condition (*he* [sic] or *they*). There were five blocks of 20 trials, run by a male experimenter who gave neither positive nor negative reinforcement. Male subjects used hostile verbs at a greater average frequency (40.38 over 100 trials) than did female subjects (35.86). The authors review previous research on use of hostile and neutral verbs in an operant conditioning technique.

GLESER, GOLDINE C., LOUIS A. GOTTSCHALK, AND JOHN WATKINS.
   "The Relationship of Sex and Intelligence to Choice of Words: A Normative Study of
   Verbal Behavior." *Journal of Clinical Psychology,* 15 (1959), 182-191.

   Samples of speech were elicited from 90 white, "occupationally adjusted, medically
healthy" subjects (most employees of Kroger Manufacturing Co.). The sample was divided
into three IQ levels (which correlated closely with education), with each group evenly
divided by sex. Each subject was asked (by a male examiner) to tell about "any interesting
or dramatic life experiences you have had." The taped responses were coded by grammatical
composition and by "psychological functions." Most IQ differences were found in
grammatical categories, while all differences in verbal behavior related to sex were found in
the psychological categories. Females used significantly more words implying feeling,
emotion, or motivation (whether positive, negative, or neutral); they also made more
references to self and used more auxiliary words and negations. Men used significantly more
words implying time, space, quantity, and destructive action. There was a tendency (not
statistically significant) for sex differences to disappear in the "highest IQ" group, with the
exception of the relative frequency of words expressing emotion. The more intelligent
(better educated) women were like men in less frequent use of self-references and negation.
But the more intelligent (better educated) men were like women in using fewer references to
place or spatial relations and fewer words implying destructive action.

HALL, EDWARD T.
   The Silent Language. Doubleday, 1959.

   Hall writes that the *can* and *may* distinction in English "originally developed informally
and was linked to sex; men and boys said 'can,' women and girls 'may' " (Fawcett Premier
Third Edition, p. 120). Since *may* sounded more refined to women, they tried to push it on
men, along with the grammatical "gobbledygook" about possible and not possible, and
teachers are still trying to instill the distinction in children. As sex role distinctions diminish,
however, he says, the *may-can* distinction "now is so mixed up it's almost impossible to
develop any rules," and either is applicable in many situations. He cites no references for his
claims.

HIRSCHMAN, LYNETTE.
   "Analysis of Supportive and Assertive Behavior in Conversations." Paper presented at
   meeting of Linguistic Society of America, July, 1974.

   Probing sex differences in conversational assertiveness and supportiveness, Hirschman
had pairs of subjects discuss a question for ten minutes (there was a total of four single-sex
and eight mixed-sex conversations). In terms of word choice, the data were analyzed for
presence of qualifiers (like *maybe, sort of, I think, I guess*), taken to accompany less
conversational assertiveness; for frequency of fillers (*uhm, well, like, you know*) indicative
of less fluent speech; frequency of affirmative words (*yeah, right, mm hmm*) indicating
supportiveness (a positive response to the other's statements). The only striking female-male

difference in word choice was in use of *mm hmm*: females outnumbered males 53 to 8, and every woman produced more *mm hmm*'s than any of the males, in fact, more than all the males put together. In the case of *yeah* (also interpreted as an affirmative word), one male accounted for almost 70% of the male total; otherwise the sexes were about the same in using this word, as they were in the use of *right,* and in the frequency of affirmative words in general. Although *mm hmm, yeah,* and *right* all are used to indicate the listener's attention, understanding, or agreement, *yeah* and *right* have more freedom of distribution than *mm hmm* (they can appear alone, at the beginning, middle, or end of an utterance; in strings of affirmatives [*right right yeah*] ; and after an interjection; while *mm hmm* is more restricted). For the speaker, hearing an *mm hmm* is a good indication that the other person isn't going to say anything more, while *yeah* or *right* are more likely to lead directly into an utterance. *Mm hmm* is conversationally less obtrusive. It was also found that females use more *mm hmm*'s in female-female conversations than in mixed-sex conversations. There was also a sex difference in the use of *I think;* males used it almost twice as much as females (118 to 66). *I think* correlated with word output (it was used more by the more assertive speakers); in these conversations, *I think* seemed to function not so much as a qualifier as a polite way of stating an opinion. [*See IV-A, IV-D, VIII-B.*]

HIRSCHMAN, LYNETTE.
   "Female-Male Differences in Conversational Interaction." Paper presented at meeting of Linguistic Society of America, Dec., 1973.

In Hirschman's sample of six dyadic conversations, females used a much higher percentage of fillers (e.g. *uhm, you know*) than males. No differences were found in the proportion of qualifiers (e.g. *maybe, probably, I think, I guess*) used, though different speakers did use different kinds of qualifiers: a female used many of the *I think, I'd say* type, while a male used many of the *most, many* type. Females more often used pronouns involving the other speaker than they used third-person references; the reverse pattern was true for males. Females used the *mm hmm* response much more often than males, particularly with each other. [*See IV-A, IV-B, IV-D, IV-E.*]

JESPERSEN, OTTO.
   "The Woman," Chapter XIII of *Language: Its Nature, Development and Origin.* London: Allen & Unwin, 1922, pp. 237-254.

(1) Word choice: according to Jespersen, women are euphemistic, exercising "a great and universal influence on linguistic development through their instinctive shrinking from coarse and gross expressions and their preference for refined and (in certain spheres) veiled and indirect expressions" (p. 246). While men swear, women use euphemistic substitutes (e.g. men say *hell;* women say *the other place*). Through the invention and use of slang (which Jespersen calls a "secondary sexual characteristic"), men are the "chief renovators of language." "This is not invalidated by the fact that quite recently, with the rise of the feminist movement, many young ladies have begun to imitate their brothers in that as well as in other respects" (p. 248). (2) Vocabulary: Jespersen claims that women's vocabulary is less extensive, and more in the central field of language (avoiding the bizarre) than is that of men, and that "men take greater interest in words as such and in their acoustic properties" (pp. 248-249). (3) Adverbs: women are "fond" of hyperbole, using more adverbs of intensity *(awfully, pretty, terribly nice, quite, so).* (4) Sentence construction: "Women

much more often than men break off without finishing their sentences, because they start talking without having thought out what they are going to say" (p. 250). The sexes, Jespersen claims, have different ways of building sentences: men use more intricate structures, with clause within clause (like a set of Chinese boxes); women add on clauses (building sentences like stringing pearls), the gradation between ideas marked not grammatically, but "emotionally," by stress and intonation. [See I, V, VI.]

KEY, MARY RITCHIE.
   "Linguistic Behavior of Male and Female." *Linguistics,* 88 (Aug. 15, 1972), 15-31.

Females may more often use the intensifiers, *so, such, quite, vastly* ("It was *so* interesting"; "I had *such* fun"). Key refers to Shuy's claim that females are more sensitive than males to indicators of lower status, and are less likely to use syntactic features with such connotations. [See I, II-A-1, III-B-3.]

KRAMER, CHERIS.
   "Folklinguistics." *Psychology Today,* 8 (June, 1974), 82-85.

Kramer discusses and compares stereotypes of female and male speech (as depicted in *New Yorker* cartoons) with differences found in actual speech in an experimental study. Kramer analyzed 156 cartoons containing adult human speech, from 13 consecutive issues (in 1973) of *The New Yorker.* In addition, she had 25 male and 25 female students indicate, for each caption, whether they thought the speaker was male or female (there was clear consensus in their choices). In the cartoons, male characters swear more freely than female characters (the student raters commented that, in general, profanity and harsh language distinguish male from female speech, and that men use a simpler, more direct, more assertive type of language, while women tend to "flower up" their remarks). Adjectives (such as *nice* and *pretty*), which are popularly associated with female speech, sometimes serve in the cartoons to identify a woman as having traditional ideas about the female role; at other times such adjectives are the basis for a joke (especially when a woman uses them while talking about a "masculine" topic); occasionally, male cartoon figures use these adjectives to indicate role reversal. Kramer emphasizes that folk-linguistics, as shown in the cartoons and the student responses, may not fit empirical data about the way people talk. She designed an experiment to explore generalizations often made: that men use a greater variety of words; that women use more adverbs ending in *-ly;* that women are more interested in people, and men in objects. The participants (17 men and 17 women) were shown two photographs, one of people and the other of a building, and asked to write paragraphs describing them. Analysis of these written descriptions indicated *no significant sex differences.* Men did not use a greater variety of prenominal adjectives; women did not use a significantly larger number of *-ly* adverbs, nor did women use more words in describing either the people or the building. Kramer then had 11 female students examine a random sample of the typed paragraphs (5 by women, 5 by men) and try to identify the sex of the writer; in all there were 59 correct guesses, and 51 incorrect ones. Kramer notes that this study was limited to written language, to essays written for a general audience, and to college freshmen—all of which may have bearing on the findings. She concludes that in communication research, "beliefs about sex-related language differences may be as important as the actual differences. As long as women play a subordinate role, their speech will be stereotyped as separate and unequal" (p. 85). [See IV-B, IV-D, IV-F.]

KRAMER, CHERIS.
"Stereotypes of Women's Speech: The Word From Cartoons." *Journal of Popular Culture,* in press.

Expanding the study of cartoons to include samples from *Ladies Home Journal, Playboy,* and *Cosmopolitan,* as well as *The New Yorker,* Kramer gave university students lists of cartoon captions and asked them to assign each caption to a male or female speaker and to give reasons for their decisions. Sex of the speaker of the captions was clearly stereotyped in more than three-fourths of the cartoons. Students of both sexes characterized stereotyped women's speech as being "stupid, vague, emotional, confused, and wordy"; men's speech was stereotyped as logical, concise, businesslike, in control. In the world of cartoons, women's speech is weaker than men's speech in emphasis, with fewer uses of exclamations and curse words. Often male speakers are putting down another person, while often when the woman talks, it is her speech itself that is the joke. Women are restricted both in how they talk and in where they talk. Women, who are found in fewer places than male speakers in the cartoons, were "seldom shown otherwise than as housewife, mother, sex object. Statements that indicated the speaker held an authoritarian position were attributed to men. Women's statements were defined primarily by personality traits rather than by professional occupation." [*See IV-D*].

KRAMER, CHERIS.
"Women's Speech: Separate But Unequal?" *Quarterly Journal of Speech,* 60 (Feb., 1974), 14-24. Reprinted in Barrie Thorne and Nancy Henley, eds., *Language and Sex: Difference and Dominance.* Rowley, Mass.: Newbury House, 1975.

Complete word taboos for one sex or the other are probably rare in English; most differences appear to be a matter of context and frequency, e.g., women knowing but not using swear words in the same context or with the same frequency as men, or women using words like *pretty, cute,* and *oh dear* in contexts and frequencies which differ from men. Men may have a claim not only on swear words, but on slang words in general. In his preface to the *Dictionary of American Slang* (New York: Thomas Y. Crowell, 1960), Flexner claims that "most American slang is created and used by males. Many types of slang words—including the taboo and strongly derogatory ones, those referring to sex, women, work, money, whiskey, politics, transportation, sports, and the like—refer primarily to male endeavor and interest. The majority of entries in this dictionary could be labeled "primary masculine use'" (p. xii). [*What if a woman compiled a dictionary of slang, and paid attention to women's speech, including that of all-female groups? Are these studies biased?*] Several sources, including Jespersen, claim women use more hyperbole than men, especially the intensive *so* (which Lakoff suggests can be used like a tag-question to avoid full commitment to a statement; Kramer notes that "since being emphatic is not seemingly a characteristic of women's speech, it would be useful to determine in what situations and with what topics women do use the intensive *so*"). Jokes and novels allude to a "syntactic looseness in women's speech"; Jespersen claims women are prone to jump from one idea to another, and not to complete sentences; Mary Ellman (*Thinking About Women,* New York: Harcourt, Brace & World, 1968) writes of the stereotyped formlessness of women's speech as represented in the writing of men like Joyce, Sartre, Mailer, and Hemingway. These stereotypes suggest areas for emprical research. One could also examine the written work of men and women to see if the dialogue is different for the sexes in novels, and if women writers treat dialogue differently. [*See I, III-A, III-B-2, IV-A, IV-C, VIII-C.*]

LAKOFF, ROBIN.
 "Language and Woman's Place." *Language in Society,* 2 (1973), 45-79.

Women have a distinctive style of speech which avoids strong statements and has connotations of uncertainty and triviality. A woman who wants to be taken seriously learns to adopt male ("neutral") vocabulary and style of speech. Specifics: (1) There are, Lakoff claims, differences between the sexes in choice and frequency of lexical items, e.g. women make far more precise discriminations in naming colors, and the domains where women have elaborate vocabularies are of little concern to men, and have a connotation of triviality. (2) Use of non-referent particles: the sexes use different expletives; women are more likely to say *oh dear, goodness,* or *fudge,* while the men use stronger expletives *(shit, damn).* Hence, men are allowed stronger means of expression than are open to women, which further reinforces men's position of strength in the real world (men are listened to with more deference). (3) Adjective choice: females are more likely to use adjectives like *adorable, charming, lovely, divine;* male or "neutral" adjectives include *great, terrific, neat.* The women's words suggest that the referent is frivolous, trivial, unimportant to the world at large. (4) Syntax: women more often use tag questions ("John is here, isn't he?" as opposed to the direct question form, "Is John here?") The tag form is midway between an outright statement and a yes-no question; it is used when the speaker is stating a claim but lacks full confidence in the truth of that claim; it gives the addressee leeway, not forcing him or her to go along with the views of the speaker. This is another way in which women's speech patterns avoid making strong statements. Women are also more likely to couch wishes in the form of requests (while men more often use commands)—another way in which women's language sounds more "polite" than men's, avoiding imposing views or claims on the addressee. [*See I, II-A-1, III-B-3, V, VII.*]

PEI, MARIO.
 Words in Sheep's Clothing. New York: Hawthorn Books, 1969.

Pei sets out to catalogue "weasel words"—words whose "semantics are deliberately changed or obscured, to achieve a specific purpose," or which are used "for the sole purpose of impressing and bamboozling the reader or hearer." He jumps from Madison Avenue to the world of moving pictures, arts, journalism, science, politics, and touches on the language of women in Chapter 5, "Debs, Mods, and Hippies" [*note the grouping in which women are placed.*] He describes female terms of address *(honey, sweetie, you're a doll, darling)* and complains, "What women use among themselves is their own business, but must they inflict it on us?" [*He apparently assumes an all-male readership.*] Pei claims that there is a "special feminine vocabulary" in English, that men "may not, dare not, and will not use." The vocabulary is characterized by abbreviation, and a "feminine diminutive suffix": *hanky, panties, nightie, meanie, cutie.* It includes French borrowings, e.g. for color names like *beige, mauve, taupe* (words which "normally mean nothing to men"). Women use more extravagant adjectives *(wonderful, heavenly, divine, dreamy).* Pei traces to "feminine influence" the use of *fun* as an adjective ("a fun dress"); the suffix *-ette (majorette),* and the prefix *mini-* ("miniskirt"). Pei concludes that feminine (and teen-age) language are meant to "proclaim that their user is a member of a certain class, and to flaunt the word-slogan like a battle-flag in the faces of mere men or of the older generation." He concludes, "a thoroughly male and adult vocabulary" [*note again the grouping*] "could form the subject of a chapter, too; but then our book might be banned in Boston."

SHUSTER, JANET.
"Grammatical Forms Marked for Male and Female in English." Unpublished (graduate student) paper (9 pp.), Dept. of Anthropology, Univ. of Chicago, 1973.

Shuster points to a usage of active vs. passive voice, and transitive vs. intransitive verbs, which is differentially marked for men's and women's speech. (1) In the following verb usages, passive forms are more common if females are speaking or being referred to: *to be laid, to be fucked, to be taken* (sexually), *to be had* (sexually), *to come across* (perform sexually), *to* (be) *put out* (sexually), *to be walked*. Active forms are more common if males are speaking or being referred to: *to lay, to fuck, to take* (sexually), *to have* (sexually), *to put* (her) *out, to walk* (her). (2) Intransitive verb forms are more often used in reference to females, or by female speakers: *fuck with him, walk home with him, go with him* on a date, *make love with him, marry with him*. Transitive forms are more common in male speech or in reference to male speakers: *fuck her, walk her home, take her out* on a date, *make love to her, marry to her*. These nonreciprocal grammatical forms express the asymmetrical power relationship of men over women. Shuster examines the active/transitive, passive/intransitive verb complexes in the speech and discourse about three characters in Mailer's novel, *Deer Park*. Dorothea, an independent woman respected by men, uses and is referred to by male forms of speech ("guys I've had for a one-night stand"). Elena and Lulu fit female stereotypes (weak; dependent on men), and male speakers refer to them as objects to be acted upon (man referring to Lulu: "I was able to take her again").

SWACKER, MARJORIE.
"The Sex of the Speaker as a Sociolinguistic Variable." In Barrie Thorne and Nancy Henley, eds., *Language and Sex: Difference and Dominance*. Rowley, Mass.: Newbury House, 1975.

Swacker had 34 informants (17 men and 17 women, all Caucasians, in their early 20's, and students) look at 3 pictures by Albrecht Dürer, and describe what he or she saw, taking as much time as needed for the description, and trying to leave nothing out. The responses were tape recorded, and results analyzed for sex differences in speaking patterns. There were distinctions in *verbosity*, with men on the average speaking for longer intervals than women. Men used considerably more *numerals* in their descriptive passages (e.g., counting as part of their description; no women counted). Women preceded half of their numerals with indicators of approximation (" . . . about six books"); only one man used a term of estimation. The sexes differed in *topic shift* markers. Both used pause patterns to mark shifts; women used significantly more conjunctions than did men, while men (but no women) used interjections to mark topic shifts (" . . . a small shelf with some books piled up on it—*OK*—the man seems to be wearing a great big robe . . . "). [*See IV-D, IV-G.*]

TUCKER, SUSIE I.
Protean Shape: A Study in Eighteenth-Century Vocabulary and Usage. London: Athlone Press, 1967.

Chapter II ("Censure and Protest") describes 18th century language practices greeted with disapproval by critics like Dr. Johnson—e.g., foreign words, affectations, cant, sailors' language, and "women's usage" (pp. 78-80). Tucker notes that the critics would have put women speakers low down in the scale of good, or desirable speech, not because they were uneducated, but because women had "particular vogue words." One commentator referred to the ladies "whose main ornaments to their correspondence were an ah! and an oh!" Mrs. Piozzi, a woman writer, was criticized for overuse of *such, so,* and *somehow,* and the indefinite *one ("one,"* Tucker notes, "pinpoints a deficiency of English, a singular common gender pronoun corresponding to *they"* p. 79). Another female writer was criticized for the indiscriminate use of *fine* ("a fine sense of honor"), and another, for her affected use of *mentally* ("she mentally preferred").

WARSHAY, DIANA W.
    "Sex Differences in Language Style." In Constantina Safilios-Rothschild, ed., *Toward a Sociology of Women.* Lexington, Mass.: Xerox College Pub., 1972, pp. 3-9.

Warshay had 263 white, middle-class students in a midwestern university respond to the Important Events Test (writing down events in the past important to them). These language samples were analyzed for differences in grammar (ratio of verb to noun forms of reference to events), content analysis, and word counts. Warshay found that, compared with females, males tended to write with less fluency, to refer to events in a verb (rather than noun) phrase, to make more time references (of a vague sort; females gave more specific dates). Males also tended to involve themselves more in their references to events (while females referred more to others), to locate the event in their personal sphere of activity (while females located events in their interacting community), and to refer less to others. "Thus the male is shown to be more active, more ego-involved in what he does, and less concerned about others. His achievements are personal, underscoring and rewarding his individuality." The female adult "exhibits concern with 'being.' Blocked or largely excluded from public achievement, she seeks satisfaction in primary relations in the local community" (p. 8).

WOOD, MARION M.
    "The Influence of Sex and Knowledge of Communication Effectiveness on Spontaneous Speech." *Word,* 22, No. 1-2-3 (1966), 112-137.

This is an experimental study varying sex of speaker (18 subjects of each sex were individually tested), stimuli evoking spontaneous speech (speakers were asked to describe photographs of the same person with different facial expressions), sex of person spoken to, and knowledge of communication effectiveness (subjects were given different sets of "pseudofeedback" about success and failure). Interaction between speaker and hearer was limited to speech by the speaker (i.e., it was one-way, with no nonverbal communication). There were quantitative findings (men had greater verbal output) and findings about sex differences in speech style and word choice. "The analysis of the 90,000-word corpus of spontaneous speech . . . revealed distinctive styles of approach for men and women. A chi-square test showed (1) a correlation between the male utterances studied and an empirical style of speech, characterized by descriptions of observable features with objectively oriented concepts, and (2) a correlation between the female utterances studied and a creative style of speech, characterized by interpretive descriptions of associate images with predominantly connotative concepts." The author suggests an "intuitive" link between these two styles and the role differentiation Robert F. Bales *(Interaction Process Analysis,* Cambridge, Mass.: Addison-Wesley, 1950), and others posit in small experimental groups (task-oriented, instrumental roles, linked to males; and socio-emotional roles tied to females). Wood also looked at specific lexical sets associated with each sex, drawing on the speech of 3 of the male and 3 of the female subjects. This analysis suggested that some words seemed more associated with males: nouns such as *background, centimeter, dots, fraction,* and *V-shape;* and verbs such as *intersect, joins, parallels, protruded,* and *right-triangular.* Only one-third of the female-exclusive lexical selections were words of this type. The female list was instead characterized by nouns such as *bird, cheese, death, family,* and *spinach;* verbs like *enjoying, gotten up, might be posing, might have just put,* and *has been surprised;* and modifiers such as *confused, distasteful, peek-a-boo, questioning,* and *skeptical.* Females varied verb tenses and used more active than passive voice, compared with men. [*See IV-D.*]

III. PHONOLOGY

A. *Phonetic Variants*

ANSHEN, FRANK.
    "Speech Variation Among Negroes in a Small Southern Community." Unpublished Ph.D. dissertation, New York Univ., 1969.

    Anshen studied phonological variables (e.g., postvocalic *r*; pronunciation of *th* as in *this;* the suffix *-in* vs. *-ing*) in the black population of Hillsboro, North Carolina. Among his findings: women use fewer stigmatized forms than men, and, compared with men, women are more sensitive to the prestige pattern.

FARB, PETER.
    Word Play: What Happens When People Talk. New York: Alfred A. Knopf, 1973.

    In a general discussion of sociolinguistic literature concerning sex differences, Farb refers to the studies [*cited in this section*] of Labov, Trudgill, and Fischer, which indicate that, at least phonologically, "women (compared with men of the same age, social class, and level of education) speak in ways which more closely resemble the prestige way of talking" (p. 51). Farb reiterates Trudgill's explanation for this phenomenon. [*See II-A-1, II-B, III-B-2, V.*]

FASOLD, RALPH W.
    "A Sociolinguistic Study of the Pronunciation of Three Vowels in Detroit Speech." Washington, D.C.: Center for Applied Linguistics, mimeo, 1968.

    Using data from the Detroit Dialect Study, Fasold found that the fronting of three vowels, /æ/, /a/, and /ɔ/, was more characteristic of lower-middle-class speakers than of upper-middle-class or working-class speakers. He also found that, especially in the lower-middle-class, women outscored men in the fronting of all three vowels. Younger informants predominated in fronting these vowels.

FISCHER, JOHN L.
"Social Influences on the Choice of a Linguistic Variant." *Word,* 14 (1958), 47-56.
Reprinted in Dell Hymes, ed., *Language in Culture and Society.* New York: Harper &
Row, 1964, pp. 483-488.

Analyzing recorded interviews with 24 children (half of each sex, ages 3-10) in a
semi-rural New England village, Fischer found variations in the use of -*in* and -*ing* as verb
endings. While all of the children used both forms to some extent, "a markedly greater
number of girls used -*ing* more frequently, while more boys used more -*in.*" Hence, in this
community "-*ing* is regarded as symbolizing female speakers and -*in* as symbolizing males."
There was a slight tendency for -*ing* to be associated with higher socio-economic status.
Personality was also a factor; a boy regarded as "model" used the -*ing* ending almost
exclusively; a boy seen as "typical" used -*in* more than half the time. There were situational
differences; -*ing* was used in more formal, and -*in* in more informal interviews. Finally, more
"formal" verbs *(criticizing, correcting, reading)* were associated with the -*ing* pronunciation,
and more informal verbs with the -*in* variant *(punchin, flubbin, swimmin).*

HAUGEN, EINAR.
" 'Sexism' and the Norwegian Language." Paper presented at Society for the
Advancement of Scandinavian Study meeting, 1974.

Referring to Scandinavian materials, Haugen summarizes various studies of language
variation by sex. Magnes Oftedal analyzed local dialects in Norway and observed greater
"carefulness" in speech of women, a trait he attributes to the greater vulnerability of
women to severe judgments about their behavior, especially their "moral" behavior. Females
tend to adopt urban expressions in preference to rural ones, and, Oftedal says, women are
usually about one generation ahead of men in linguistic development. Anders Steinsholt
made similar observations: in urbanizing areas women use a more urban dialect than their
sons, and "it is almost a rule that the members of a family divide into three groups
linguistically: the father in one, the sons in one, and the mother and daughters in a third."
While women go on adapting their language, men stop changing their language by age 30.
Steinsholt attributes this to the greater demands made on proper female behavior. In a study
of linguistic innovations in an urbanizing rural community in Denmark, Anker Jensen
reported a similar finding in 1892: the women were ahead of the men in adopting urban
speech patterns. In a study in French Switzerland, Gauchat made the same finding in 1905.
[*See III-A-1.*]

KRAMER, CHERIS.
"Women's Speech: Separate But Unequal?" *Quarterly Journal of Speech,* 60 (Feb.,
1974), 14-24. Reprinted in Barrie Thorne and Nancy Henley, eds., *Language and
Sex: Difference and Dominance.* Rowley, Mass.: Newbury House, 1975.

Kramer reviews research indicating that women are more likely than men to use phonetic
forms considered correct (research by Shuy; Shuy, Wolfram, and Riley; Fischer; Labov;
Levine and Crockett). [*See I, II-B, III-B-2, IV-A, IV-C, VIII-C.*]

LABOV, WILLIAM.
   Sociolinguistic Patterns. Philadelphia: Univ. of Pennsylvania Press, 1972, pp. 243;
   301-304.

   In careful speech women use fewer stigmatized forms than men and are more sensitive
than men to prestige patterns; lower-middle-class women show the most extreme form of
this behavior. There are implications for the role of women in furthering linguistic change.
Writing in 1905, L. Gauchat reported that in Paris, women used more of the newer linguistic
forms than men did. Recent studies in New York (see William Labov, *The Social
Stratification of English in New York City,* Washington, D.C.: Center for Applied
Linguistics, 1966), Detroit (research of Shuy, Wolfram, and Riley), and Chicago (Labov's
research) also show that women use the most advanced forms in their casual speech, and
correct more sharply to the other extremes in their formal speech. Women do not, however,
always lead in the course of linguistic change; Labov's study of Martha's Vineyard found
male speakers carried some new forms; Trudgill suggests that in Norwich, men lead in the
use of new vernacular forms in casual speech. "The correct generalization then is not that
women lead in linguistic change, but rather that the sexual differentiation of speech often
plays a major role in the mechanism of linguistic evolution." [*See VII.*]

LEVINE, LEWIS AND HARRY J. CROCKETT, JR.
   "Speech Variation in a Piedmont Community: Postvocalic *r.*" In Stanley Lieberson,
   ed., *Explorations in Sociolinguistics.* The Hague: Mouton, 1966, 76-98.

   The authors studied speech variation and social structure in a North Carolina Piedmont
community, interviewing 275 white residents to elicit word pronunciations. Pronunciation
of the postvocalic *r* (as in *bare*) varied by age, length of residence in the community,
occupation and education, and sex. Females were more likely than males to pronounce the
postvocalic *r* (i.e., to use the more "correct" form), as were those of higher education, those
in prestigeful occupations, newer community residents, and younger people. These groups
may "spearhead" linguistic change, as the community shifts to the national norm. On the
other hand, there may be a difference in points of reference, with these groups taking the
national norm as their speech model, while "the linguistic behavior of males, older people,
long-term residents, and blue-collar respondents is referred to a Southern prestige norm–the
r-less pronunciation of the coastal plain."

SHUY, ROGER W., WALTER A. WOLFRAM, AND WILLIAM K. RILEY.
   Linguistic Correlates of Social Stratification in Detroit Speech. Final Report, Project
   6-1347. Washington, D.C.: U.S. Office of Education, 1967.

   This extensive study of the speech of 700 randomly selected Detroit residents correlated
linguistic and social variables, including sex. With some variation by class, women showed
greater sensitivity than men to multiple negation and pronominal apposition (as in "my
brother *he* went to the park"). Males had a greater tendency to use nasalized vowels, e.g.
/mǣ/ for *man,* and to use -*in* rather than -*ing* (supporting Fischer's findings).

TRUDGILL, PETER.
　　"Sex, Covert Prestige, and Linguistic Change in the Urban British English of Norwich." *Language in Society,* 1 (1972), 179-195. Reprinted in Barrie Thorne and Nancy Henley, eds., *Language and Sex: Difference and Dominance.* Rowley, Mass.: Newbury House, 1975.

　　Trudgill reviews studies and presents his own data for speakers of urban British English in Norwich, showing that "women, allowing for other variables such as age, education and social class, consistently produce linguistic forms which more closely approach those of the standard language or have higher prestige than those produced by men, or, alternatively, that they produce forms of this type more frequently." He offers several "speculative" explanations for this finding: (1) Women are more status-conscious than men; their insecure and subordinate social position makes it "more necessary for women to secure and signal their social status linguistically and in other ways." Men can be rated socially by their occupation, by what they *do,* while women are rated on how they *appear* – hence reliance on non-occupational signals of status, such as speech. (2) Working-class speech and culture have connotations of masculinity, being associated with roughness and toughness, while refinement and sophistication are considered feminine characteristics. In a sometimes covert way, men value non-standard speech as a signal of masculinity and of group solidarity. Trudgill found an age difference: males of all ages, and females under 30, valued non-standard speech forms more than females over 30. In terms of linguistic change, standard forms are introduced by middle-class women, and non-standard forms by working-class men.

WOLFRAM, WALTER A.
　　A Sociolinguistic Description of Detroit Negro Speech. Washington, D.C.: Center for Applied Linguistics, 1969.

　　Wolfram drew on data from the Detroit Dialect Study (reported in Shuy, Wolfram, and Riley, 1967) to include more linguistic variables, and with a focus on the black population. He found that within each social class, black females approximated the standard English norm more than males. Females of all classes had fewer *f, t,* or $\emptyset$ realizations of *th* (as in *tooth*); females more often pronounced final consonant clusters (as in *friend*) and the postvocalic *r* (as in *car*).

B. Suprasegmentals

1. General

ADDINGTON, D. W.
　　"The Relationship of Selected Vocal Characteristics to Personality Perception." *Speech Monographs,* 35 (1968), 492-503.

　　Addington used an experiment to explore whether male and female speakers using the same vocal characteristics elicit different personality perception. Two male and two female trained speakers alternately made their voices more breathy, tense, thin, flat, throaty, nasal, and orotund; they also varied rate and pitch. Students listened to tapes of these voice variations and described the speaker's personality. Factor analysis of the results indicated that "changes in male voice affect personality perception differently than do similar changes in female voices" (497); female vocal manipulations altered personality ascriptions more than those of males. For example, increased thinness of voice quality had no effect on perception of males, but for female voices elicited perceptions of increased social, physical, emotional, and mental immaturity; also more sensitivity and sense of humor. Males using increased vocal tension were perceived as being older, more unyielding, and cantankerous, while females were seen as younger, more emotional, feminine, high-strung, and less intelligent. Increased throatiness in male speakers led to their being stereotyped as older, more realistic, mature, sophisticated, and well adjusted. Females with more throaty voices were seen as "cloddish or oafish" (less intelligent, lazier, more boorish, ugly, sickly, careless, etc.).

AUSTIN, WILLIAM M.
   "Some Social Aspects of Paralanguage." *Canadian Journal of Linguistics,* 11 (1965), 31-39.

   Paralanguage is defined as significant noises, in a code situation between sender and receiver, made by the non-articulated vocal tract (any articulations tend to be stylistic variants). Vocal modifiers, one paralinguistic category, indicate changes in the vocal tract only; one vocal modifier is in the oral/nasal distinction. "In our culture little boys tend to be nasal . . . and little girls, oral. Nasality is considered 'tough' and 'vulgar' and somewhat discouraged by elders. 'Gentlemanly' little boys tend to be oral also." Certain signals are highly suggestive of "paramorphology": "A 'little girl's voice' (innocence, helplessness, regression) is composed of high pitch and orality." In the paralanguage of courtship, the male is low and nasal, the female high, oral and giggling; in the final stages of courtship speech, it is low and nasal in both, but with "wide pitch and intensity variation on the part of the female." Derogatory imitation, "one of the most infuriating acts of aggression one person can commit on another," is illustrated for both male and female, with mention of the "even stronger" case in which "male or female imitates a male with derogatory female imitation." For upper-class paralanguage, Austin writes, it must be clear, low, and oral in men; and clear and oral, with a choice of high or low for women. "Low pitch has lately become fashionable for women, but fifty years ago all 'ladies' spoke with a high pitch." Japanese speech has both marked linguistic differences between male and female, and striking paralinguistic differences: males loud and low, "in Samurai movies almost a bark"; females soft and high, almost a squeak.

CRYSTAL, D.
   "Prosodic and Paralinguistic Correlates of Social Categories." In Edwin Ardener, ed., *Social Anthropology and Language.* London: Tavistock, 1971, pp. 185-206.

   Crystal calls attention, in a general way, to the non-segmental phonetic and phonological characteristics of speech: pitch, loudness, speed of utterance, and use of qualities of voice such as nasalization or breathiness in order to communicate specific meanings. He claims that non-segmental phonology is "one of the main ways of establishing the identity of social groups in speech," and notes that non-segmental features have been found to correlate with sex, age, status, occupation, and speech genres. "Intuitive impressions of effeminacy in English, for example, partly correlate with segmental effects such as lisping, but are mainly non-segmental; a 'simpering' voice, for instance, largely reduces to the use of a wider pitch-range than normal (for men), with *glissando* effects between stressed syllables, a more frequent use of complex tones (e.g., the fall-rise and the rise-fall), the use of breathiness and huskiness in the voice, and switching to a higher (falsetto) register from time to time." Crystal cites data from other languages about non-segmental correlates of sex. He also suggests that *responses* to non-segmental vocal effects can be a valuable part of a description; for example, in Mohave the breaking of the male voice in adolescence is not considered an important or relevant indication of puberty, whereas in English it is.

LAVER, JOHN D. M.
   "Voice Quality and Indexical Information." *British Journal of Disorders of Communication,* 33 (1968), 43-54.

   Laver outlines a descriptive model of voice quality (which is determined by anatomy and voluntary muscular "setting," and includes variations in phonation type, pitch range, and loudness range of laryngeal setting, and supralaryngeal modifications, such as nasalization). Voice quality is an index to biological, psychological, and social characteristics of the speaker. Laver includes "sex and age" under "biological information about the speaker": "One usually forms fairly accurate impressions, from voice quality alone, of a speaker's sex and age . . . Deviations from 'normal' expectations about the correlation between a speaker's voice and his sex and age seem to have a powerful effect on impressions of personality" (p. 49). Several references are included to support these statements.

2. Pitch

FARB, PETER.
   Word Play: What Happens When People Talk. New York: Alfred A. Knopf, 1973.

   Drawing on Crystal's comments about sex differences in voice types [*see annotation in III-B-1*], Farb notes that in English-speaking communities, some women are said to have "sexy voices," and some men are said to sound "effeminate" (the common explanation is that this involves a lisp). The effeminate voice has a wider pitch range than the male norm; it uses sliding effects between stressed syllables, has more breathiness in voice quality, and uses complex tonal patterns. [*See II-A-1, II-B, III-A, V.*]

HENNESSEE, JUDITH.
   "Some News Is Good News." *Ms.,* 3 (July, 1974), 25-29.

   Reporting on the experiences of female TV news reporters, Hennessee comments on the presumed relationship between a low-pitched voice and credibility. In American culture the norm for an authoritative voice is male; "higher-pitched voices are still associated with unpleasantness, evoking nagging mothers or wives, waspish schoolteachers, acerbic librarians." (In France, women's voices are preferred for news broadcasting.) Yet a survey of attitudes toward television newswomen, done by researchers at the Univ. of Wisconsin, showed that "only about one-fifth of those polled (a sample which included small-town conservative families) said they would be more likely to believe a news report by a man.

Newswomen, it appears, have more support from their viewers than from their employers." Women newscasters with the deepest voices are sometimes called the most authoritative of women in TV news.

KRAMER, CHERIS.
"Women's Speech: Separate But Unequal?" *Quarterly Journal of Speech,* 60 (Feb., 1974), 14-24. Reprinted in Barrie Thorne and Nancy Henley, eds., *Language and Sex: Difference and Dominance.* Rowley, Mass.: Newbury House, 1975.

Kramer comments upon cultural stereotypes about the pitch level of women's speech. In cartoons and novels the talk of all-female gatherings is loud and high-pitched (Kramer suggests a research question: "Do women change volume and pitch, depending on the situation and the ratio of men and women present?"). High pitch is a stereotyped attribute of females; on Sesame Street boy monsters are "brave and gruff" and girl monsters are "high-pitched and timid" (cited from Letty Cottin Pogrebin, "Down with Sexist Upbringing," *Ms.,* 1 [Spring, 1972], p. 28). People do not associate the higher-pitched voice with serious topics—a reason broadcasters give for not employing female news announcers. Kramer suggests researching the response of each sex to women's voices, and studying whether women with broadcasting jobs change their pitch and volume for performance on the air more than male broadcasters. "At what age does this preference for the male voice begin? And in what situations other than broadcasting?" [*See I, II-B, III-A, IV-A, IV-C, VIII-C.*]

LIEBERMAN, PHILIP.
Intonation, Perception, and Language. Cambridge: M.I.T. Press, 1967.

Lieberman cites a study of the vocalizations of a 10-month-old boy and a girl of 13 months which found that the average fundamental frequency of the babies' vocalizations was 50-100 cps lower when they were "talking" with their fathers than when they were "talking" with their mothers. This suggests that intonation patterns may vary with the sex spoken to (pp. 45-46).

MATTINGLY, IGNATIUS G.
"Speaker Variation and Vocal-Tract Size." Paper presented at Acoustical Society of America, 1966. Abstract in *Journal of the Acoustical Society of America,* 39 (1966), 1219.

This study tested the hypothesis that differences in the formant-frequency value sets (among speakers of the same dialect) are due chiefly to variations in individual vocal-tract size. For three speaker classes—men, women, children—the distribution of values for each of three formants of each of ten vowels was correlated with every other such distribution. If the differences were due to size of the vocal tract, the correlations should have been high, but most scores were low. Furthermore, the separation between male and female distributions for some vowel formants was much sharper than variation in individual vocal-tract size could reasonably explain. The author concludes: "The variation within class must be stylistic, not physical; and the difference between male and female formant values, though doubtless related to typical male and female vocal-tract size, is probably a linguistic convention."

SACHS, JACQUELINE.
"Cues to the Identification of Sex in Children's Speech." In Barrie Thorne and Nancy Henley, eds., *Language and Sex: Difference and Dominance.* Rowley, Mass.: Newbury House, 1975.

Prepubertal boys and girls can typically be identified as to sex from their voices. This paper presents three studies on the cues used in this identification. (1) Judges were able to guess the sex of the child from hearing isolated vowels, though not as well as from sentences. (2) Judges could not accurately determine sex from sentences played backwards, suggesting that, beyond the phonetic aspects of the voices, there is considerable information in normal sentences that carries information about the sex of the speaker. (3) When judges rated spoken sentences on semantic differential scales, a factor emerged that was correlated with the perceived masculinity or femininity of the voice, along with two other factors, Active-Passive and Fluent-Disfluent. This result suggests that there is an independent cue to the sex of the speaker that does not involve how active the voice sounds or how fluent it is. [*Author's annotation.*] [*See VII.*]

SACHS, JACQUELINE, PHILIP LIEBERMAN, AND DONNA ERICKSON.
"Anatomical and Cultural Determinants of Male and Female Speech." In Roger W. Shuy and Ralph W. Fasold, eds., *Language Attitudes: Current Trends and Prospects.* Washington, D.C.: Georgetown Univ. Press, 1973, pp. 74-84.

In the phonetic differentiation between adult male and female voices, the most obvious factor is pitch, or fundamental frequency of phonation. The lower fundamental frequencies of the male are a consequence of secondary sexual dimorphism occurring at puberty (the larynx of the male is enlarged and vocal cords become longer and thicker). There is, however, evidence that "the acoustic differences are greater than one would expect if the sole determining factor were simply the average anatomical difference that exists between adult men and women." Adult men and women "may modify their articulation of the same phonetic elements to produce acoustic signals that correspond to the male-female archetypes. In other words, men tend to talk as though they were bigger, and women as though they were smaller, than they actually may be." To explore this possibility, Sachs *et al.* studied preadolescent children (with larynxes of the same size relative to weight and height, and hence with no obvious anatomical basis for a sex difference in formant frequencies). They recorded samples of speech for 14 boys and 12 girls ranging in age from 4 to 14 years and had 83 adult judges listen to the tape and try to identify each voice as male or female. The results: "Judges could reliably and validly identify the sex of children from their voices. Boys on the average had higher fundamentals but lower formants than girls." The authors examined possible explanations: while they found no average difference in articulatory mechanism size, there may be differential use of anatomy, or there could be hormonal control over certain aspects of the motor output. Or "the children could be learning culturally determined patterns that are viewed as appropriate for each sex." A speaker could change the formant pattern, e.g., by spreading the lips to shorten the vocal tract and raise the formants ("the characteristic way some women have of talking and smiling at the same time would have just this effect"). The judges may have drawn on cues other than formant pattern to identify the sex of the child speaker, e.g., it seems that "boys had a more forceful, definite rhythm of speaking than the girls"; there may have been differences in vocabulary items and in intonation patterns. The paper suggests that pitch may not be determined totally by anatomical structure, but also by sex roles and cultural expectations. [*See VII.*]

3. Intonation

BREND, RUTH M.
  "Male-Female Intonation Patterns in American English." *Proceedings of the Seventh International Congress of Phonetic Sciences, 1971.* The Hague: Mouton, 1972, pp. 866-870. Reprinted in Barrie Thorne and Nancy Henley, eds., *Language and Sex: Difference and Dominance.* Rowley, Mass.: Newbury House, 1975.

While speakers of American English have some intonation patterns in common, certain patterns seem to be completely lacking from men's speech, while others are differently preferred by men and women. For example, men tend to use the incomplete "deliberative" pattern, i.e., the small upstep from the low ('Yes, 'yes, I/'know.), while women prefer the "more polite" incomplete longer upstep ('Yes, 'yes I 'know.). Certain patterns are used predominantly if not solely by women, e.g. the "surprise" patterns of high-low down-glides ('Oh 'that's 'awful!), the "request confirmation" pattern (You 'do!); the hesitation pattern (Well, I /'studied . . .); and the "polite, cheerful" pattern (Are you 'coming?). Furthermore, men rarely, if ever, use the highest level of pitch that women use; most men have only three contrastive levels of intonation, while many women have four.

EBLE, CONNIE C.
  "How the Speech of Some Is More Equal Than Others." Paper presented at Southeastern Conference on Linguistics, 1972.

"It is generally thought that women have more extremes of high and low intonation than do men and that there are some intonation patterns, impressionistically the 'whining, questioning, helpless' patterns, which are used predominantly by women." [*See II-B.*]

KEY, MARY RITCHIE.
  "Linguistic Behavior of Male and Female." *Linguistics,* 88 (Aug. 15, 1972), 15-31.

"It is quite likely that women use patterns of uncertainty and indefiniteness more often than men—patterns of PLIGHT" (p. 18). One of Key's students, in a brief exploratory experiment, listened to children in the 3rd, 4th, and 5th grades retell a story. "The girls spoke with very expressive intonation, and the boys toned down the intonational features, even to the point of monotony, 'playing it cool' " (p. 18). Radio and TV broadcasters are concerned with pronunciation features; one handbook for announcers concludes that women's delivery "is lacking in the authority needed for a convincing newscast." However, in Germany and in the South, women's voices are heard frequently on the air. [*See I, II-A-1, II-B.*]

LAKOFF, ROBIN.
  "Language and Woman's Place." *Language in Society,* 2 (1973), 45-79.

There is a peculiar sentence intonation pattern found in English only among women: a declarative answer to a question, but with a rising inflection typical of a yes-no question, and conveying hesitance, as though one were seeking confirmation. Example: (Q) "When will dinner be ready?" (A) [using this intonation style] "Oh . . . around six o'clock . . . ?" As though the second speaker is saying, "Six o'clock, if that's OK with you, if you agree." Speaker (A) comes out sounding insecure and unsure of her opinion. This pattern indicates the unwillingness of women to state an opinion directly. [*See I, II-A-1, II-B, V, VII.*]

SAMARIN, WILLIAM.
   Tongues of Men and Angels. New York: Macmillan, 1972.

Samarin notes sex differences in the production of glossolalia. One of his respondents commented that "men speak more forcefully as a rule, and some women have a crying or weeping tone (something I have observed as well); even voice quality may be different" (p. 96).

4. Speech Intensity

LEGMAN, G.
   Rationale of the Dirty Joke: An Analysis of Sexual Humor. Castle Books, 1968.

This extensive analysis of erotic folklore includes a section on "the voice as phallus" (pp. 336-337), which begins with a psychoanalytic argument that there is an unconscious identification of the voice as "the virile prerogative of the dominant sex." When a female "usurps" this prerogative through a powerful speaking voice or forthright self-expression, she becomes "attractively dominant to some men, and repellent (the man-eating, song-singing Siren, Harpy or Rhine-maiden) to others." She may be seen as immoral. Legman also asserts that where men are in "dominated situations, as in armies or on college faculties, very hedged and repressed ways of speech become habitual," and he notes that "the Milquetoast or Dagwood has, traditionally, a weakly faint or absurdly screeching voice." [*See II-A-1, IV-C.*]

MARKEL, NORMAN N., LAYNE D. PREBOR, AND JOHN F. BRANDT.
   "Bio-social Factors in Dyadic Communication: Sex and Speaking Intensity." *Journal of Personality and Social Psychology,* 23 (1972), 11-13.

An experimental study in which male and female subjects spoke to male and female experimenters, at near and far distances. Average speaking intensity was determined by means of a graphic level recorder. Male subjects spoke with greater intensity than females, and there was a significant interaction between sex of subjects and sex of experimenter such that all subjects decreased intensity to the same-sex experimenter and increased intensity to the opposite-sex experimenter. These results are interpreted as reflecting a greater affiliation to an experimenter of the same sex.

IV. CONVERSATIONAL PATTERNS

A. *General References*

HIRSCHMAN, LYNETTE.
   "Analysis of Supportive and Assertive Behavior in Conversations." Paper presented at meeting of Linguistic Society of America, July, 1974.

Hirschman ran two experiments, each with two female and two male subjects (all white college students, previously unacquainted). The four subjects were separated into two pairs and given a question to discuss for ten minutes (the question dealt with love, sexuality, and marriage). Pairs were rotated, producing four single-sex and eight mixed-sex conversations, which were recorded, transcribed, and analyzed. It was hypothesized that in conversational behavior females would be more supportive, and males more assertive (although supportiveness and assertiveness were not understood to be opposites; "ideally it would be possible to be simultaneously assertive and supportive"). Assertiveness was measured by patterns of obtaining and holding the floor (interrupting, talking a lot, not losing the floor to an interrupter); relative absence of qualifiers *(maybe, sort of, I think, I guess);* fluency in speech (related to frequency of fillers and ratio of clauses finished to clauses started). Supportiveness was measured by frequency of affirmative words *(yeah, right, mm hmm)* indicating positive response to the other's statements; picking up on the other's statement (e.g. using interutterance connectives like *and*); asking questions to draw out the other speaker. Data was sparse or inconclusive on some variables (interruptions, questions, utterance classification). Overall, the amount of speech, and the average percentage of word output were equal for the sexes. Differences in mean length of utterance, frequency of affirmative words, frequency of fillers, and ratio of completed to attempted clauses were not statistically significant. The only striking overall female-male difference was in the use of *mm hmm,* where females outnumbered males 53 to 8. There was also a difference in the use of *I think;* contrary to expectation, males used almost twice as many *I think*'s as females (118 to 66). Comparing same-sex with mixed-sex conversations, no significant differences were found. "There seemed to be a tendency for the subjects to use a higher frequency of affirmative words in the same-sex conversations than in the mixed-sex conversations. Also the males use fewer *I think*'s in the male-male conversations, and the females use more *mm hmm*'s." Hirschman concludes that the lack of correlation between most of the variables and sex can be interpreted in several ways: (1) the variables chosen do not represent assertiveness and supportiveness (there is some evidence to this effect, e.g. the finding that *I think* may be a more polite way of stating an opinion than a qualifier, and the fact that the more fluent people did not particularly dominate the bulk of the conversations—in several cases the less coherent speakers took many more words to communicate one idea, so their word output was high, but not their contribution in terms of content); (2) the situation did not lend itself to differences in female-male display of supportive or assertive behavior (the situation was awkward socially for the participants; the conversations were strained and generally very polite; the questions dealt with human relations, an area usually considered of more interest to females than to males); (3) the hypothesis may be incorrect; males and females may be equally supportive and equally assertive in conversational behavior. [*See II-B, VI-D, VIII-B.*]

HIRSCHMAN, LYNETTE.
"Female-Male Differences in Conversational Interaction." Paper presented at Linguistic Society of America, Dec., 1973. (Research conducted by Hirschman, Jill Gross, Jane Savitt, and Kathy Sanders.)

Two male and two female white college students (all unacquainted) were taped in dyadic conversation, in all possible pairs of the four, with topic controlled, for ten minutes per pair, giving a total of 60 minutes of tape. The conversations were analyzed for, first, certain speech characteristics: length of time each person held the floor; number of words produced by each; percent of time used for talking (by either) in each conversation; and proportion of fillers and qualifiers used. Second, some features of conversational interaction were examined: use of personal pronouns which include the other, as opposed to third person pronouns and generic collectives; affirmative and other responses to other speaker; and interruptions (successful and unsuccessful). Finally, the investigators looked at aspects of the "flow of conversation," such as initiation, elaboration, and change of topic; and asking and answering of questions. No conclusions are drawn about differences in female and male speech patterns, though the following results are reported: word-count data and that from speaking time were parallel, and the informants were neatly ordered in both. More time was used in talking, in conversations with a female present. Females had a much higher percentage of fillers than did males. No differences were found in proportion of qualifiers, though there were individual differences in types of qualifiers used, as there were other individual differences in speech styles. Females had a much greater frequency of pronouns involving the other speaker than third-person references, and males had the reverse. Females used the *mm hmm* response much more often than males, particularly with each other. The two females interrupted (or overlapped) each other more than any other pair. In "flow of conversation," the females when talking to each other tended to elaborate on each other's utterances, the males to argue; a female-question/male-answer pattern emerged in several conversations. These results aren't subject to generalization, but the study both suggests and tests some promising measures, and permits the formulation of interesting hypotheses. Hirschman suggests the above measures be used with larger samples, though with further refinement of the interruption variable. Females may talk more easily to each other than to men. Differences in style may be related to differences in assertiveness. Perhaps "voluminous female speakers compensate for their possible aggressiveness by increased indications of hesitancy and increased responsiveness." The female-question/male-answer pattern suggests a possible role of the female as facilitator of the conversation. It's also possible in examining flow of conversation that "males tend to dispute the other person's utterance or ignore it, while the females acknowledge it, or often build on it." [*See II-B, IV-B, IV-D, IV-E.*]

KRAMER, CHERIS.
"Women's Speech: Separate But Unequal?" *Quarterly Journal of Speech,* 60 (Feb., 1974), 14-24. Reprinted in Barrie Thorne and Nancy Henley, eds., *Language and Sex: Difference and Dominance.* Rowley, Mass.: Newbury House, 1975.

Kramer examines stereotypes about women's speech—about how people think women speak or should speak—as shown in etiquette manuals, speech books, cartoons, and novels, and she uses these stereotypes to suggest empirical questions to research. Kramer relates these questions to "the larger hypothesis that women's speech reflects the stereotyped role of male and female in our society, i.e., women in a subservient, nurturing position in a male-dominated world." Areas for research: (1) "great verbosity is not the prescribed behavior for females" (e.g., etiquette books advise females not to talk as much as males, to draw out males in a conversation and let them talk about themselves). Since women are not supposed to talk as much as men, perhaps a "talkative" woman is one that does talk as much as a man. Kramer suggests experiments, e.g. that measure the total amount of talking time for men and women in a variety of situations; that see if the ratio of men to women in the situation makes a difference in the relative verbosity of each sex; that measure how much talking a woman can do before she is labelled "talkative" (including types of sentence construction used, volume of voice, speech topics). (2) Do women use more questions and fewer declarative sentences than men? Do women (as Lakoff claims) actually use tag-questions more than men? Do their declarative sentences contain more qualifiers? In what situations, and on what topics? Do women, as Lakoff believes, use more polite request forms? How do such patterns relate to patterns of subordination and submission to men? (3) A stereotype of women's gatherings is that the talk is loud and high-pitched (the "hen session" stereotype, with speech called a "cackle"). Do women change volume and pitch, depending on the situation and the ratio of men and women present? The pitch of the female voice (usually higher because of physical reasons) is a stereotyped attribute of females, associated with other undesirable, but "feminine" traits, e.g., timidity, and trivial topics (a broadcaster explaining why so few U.S. television networks employ women reporters said, "As a whole, people don't like to hear women's voices telling them serious things"). One could compare women to men in attitudes to hearing women's voices over radio and television. (4) What are the speech patterns of women in positions of some power? Do "submissive" speech patterns continue? [*See I, II-B, III-A, III-B-2, IV-C, VIII-C.*]

B. Conversational Styles

ABRAHAMS, ROGER.
   "Negotiating Respect: Patterns of Presentation Among Black Women." *Journal of American Folklore,* forthcoming.

Theoretically grounded in the dramaturgical approach of Goffman, this paper presents a conceptualization of the relationship between language styles of black women and the use of such styles for the assertion of status as *women*. Abrahams argues that "the essence of . . . negotiation lies in a woman being both sweet and tough depending upon her capacity to define and reasonably manipulate the situation." Ideally she has the ability to *talk sweet* with her infants and peers, but *talk smart* with anyone who might threaten her self-image. Considerable material illustrative of black women's presentational styles and forms and their role in the maintenance of Afro-American social and cultural structures is presented. [*Annotation by Laurel Walum.*]

BERNARD, JESSIE.
   "Talk, Conversation, Listening, Silence," Chapter 6 of *The Sex Game*. New York:
   Atheneum, 1972, pp. 135-164.

Using a wide assortment of studies, anecdotes, and observations, Bernard generalizes
about how the sexes talk and converse. Experimental studies of face-to-face groups
distinguish "instrumental" talk (having to do with orientation, facts, and information) from
"expressive" talk (dealing with feelings). "Traditionally the cultural norms for femininity
and womanliness have prescribed appreciatively expressive talk or stroking for women . . .
They were to raise the status of the other, relieve tension, agree, concur, comply,
understand, accept" (p. 137). Women may ask for suggestions, directions, opinions, or
expressions of feeling, "drawing men out," and conceding dominance in talking
relationships. Instrumental talk (more associated with males) orients, and
conveys information or facts. It may involve lecturing; it may become argumentative in style
(demanding evidence and proof, and insisting that everything be based on reason or logic); it
may involve a debating style which regards all talk as a competitive sport. This conflictful
and competitive style may be particularly inhibiting to women, since women tend to be less
competitive than men. Women furthermore "tend to be handicapped in fact-anchored talk.
In circles where conversation is most likely to occur, they are usually less well educated than
the men, less likely to have a hard, factual background, less in contact with the world of
knowledge. Personality is more important; personal opinion, attitudes, and observations give
them a wider berth to move in and are therefore more important for them than facts" (p.
153). [*See IV-D, IV-G.*]

CHESLER, PHYLLIS.
   Women and Madness. New York: Doubleday, 1972.

Many dialogues between women seem "senseless" or "mindless" to men; the women
seem to be reciting monologues at each other, neither really listening to or judging what the
other is saying. But the women are approaching a kind of emotional resolution and comfort,
telling separate confessions, feelings, in parallel. Each "comments upon the other's feelings
by reflecting them in a very sensitive matching process." Their theme, method, and goal are
nonverbal; facial expressions, pauses, sighs, and seemingly unrelated responses are crucial to
such a dialogue. On its most ordinary level, this conversational sharing gives women
emotional reality and comfort they cannot find with men; on its highest level, "it
constitutes the basic tools of art and psychic awareness" (p. 268).

CONKLIN, NANCY FAIRES.
   "Perspectives on the Dialects of Women." Paper presented at American Dialect
   Society, 1973.

"No major study of language use in natural social groups has attempted to study
women's speech." Labov justifies choosing to study only male adolescent peer groups on the
grounds that males are the "chief exemplars of the vernacular culture." But there is no
conclusive evidence that women do not participate fully in the vernacular culture.
"Sociolinguistic data do *not* show that women are less 'nonstandard' in casual, relaxed,

natural speech, only that they are less likely to exhibit their most relaxed speech styles in front of a linguistic investigator, especially a male investigator, due to their extreme social sensitivity. Women's speech in natural interaction groups, especially the female-only group, which has not been investigated at all, may be quite different from the so-called 'vernacular' styles so far reported." The weekly "consciousness-raising" discussion group of the women's movement developed out of the traditional female *Kaffeeklatsch;* this may be "an interaction type specific to women," and it may be "in these natural kinds of environments, in all-female groups, contrasted with data from more public, male/female interactions, that the essence of the dialect of women may be found, and women's whole, wide range of dialectal variation be recognized." [*See II-A-2, V.*]

COSER, ROSE LAUB.
   "Laughter Among Colleagues." *Psychiatry,* 23 (1960), 81-95.

   Coser recorded all conversations in which humor and laughter occurred at staff meetings of a mental hospital for a period of three months (total of 20 meetings). The meetings were formally structured and attended by individuals of different status positions (psychiatrists, residents, paramedical staff). Coser found "the use of humor took place in such a way as to relax the rigidity of the social structure without, however, upsetting it. Those who were of higher status positions more frequently took the initiative to use humor; more significant, still, the target of a witticism, if he was present, was never in a higher authority position than the initiator" (p. 95). There was a hierarchy of joking: senior staff made witticisms more often than junior members (whereas the humor of the latter was more often directed against patients and their relatives, and against themselves). Sex differences also figured into the hierarchy of humor: "at the meetings, men made by far the more frequent witticisms—99 out of 103—but women often laughed harder" (p. 85). This was not due to fewer numbers; there were more women at the meetings than there were junior staff. This pattern, Coser suggests, is in line with a cultural expectation that women should not challenge male authority, that women should be passive and receptive rather than active and initiating. "A woman who has a good sense of humor is one who laughs (but not too loudly!) when a man makes a witticism or tells a good joke. A man who has a good sense of humor is one who is witty in his remarks and tells good jokes. The man provides; the woman receives" (p. 85). [*See IV-C.*]

FASTEAU, MARC.
   "Why Aren't We Talking?" *Ms.,* 1 (July, 1972), 16.

   Emphasizing the need for men's liberation, Fasteau criticizes the competition, the impersonality, the obstacles to communication among men. "We've been taught that 'real men' are never passive or dependent, always dominant in relationships with women or other men, and don't talk about or directly express feelings, especially feelings that don't contribute to dominance . . . There is nothing among men that resembles the personal communication that women have developed among themselves. We don't know very much about ourselves, and we know even less about each other." In his closest friendships with males, Fasteau writes, competition was a continual theme. "We always needed an excuse to talk. Getting together for its own sake would have been frightening. Talking personally and spontaneously involves revealing doubts, plans which may fail, ideas which haven't been thought through, happiness over things the other person may think trivial—in short, making ourselves vulnerable. That was too risky."

GRIER, WILLIAM H., AND PRICE M. COBBS.
   Black Rage. New York: Basic Books, 1968. (New York: Bantam, 1969).

Psychiatrists Grier and Cobbs offer a lengthy discourse on the black patois and its origins, with particular attention to its use by black men as a tool of seduction (section V of Chapter VI, pp. 96-108, Bantam edition). In their analysis, the patois from early slave times, though a product of the white masters' control of the slaves' language, has served as a bond of unity and "secret language" for blacks. They state that "the patois which was imposed as a brand of humiliation, defeat and suffering . . . has been turned to express defiance against the oppressor and, in a subtle but significant way, vanquishment of the white oppressor" (p. 107). This vanquishment is a symbolic one, acted out in their "vanquishment" of women. The authors report that a group of black men revealed, without exception, that as a technique of seduction they "reverted to the patois" at a crucial point. "Black women [according to these men] said that they experienced an intensification of excitement when their lovers reverted to the 'old language' " (p. 107). Grier and Cobbs describe several case histories of competent black men who use the patois, particularly in this way. "It is as if in his sexual conquests," they write, "the black man welcomes the opportunity to show his skill, his desirability, and his superiority over his white oppressor in the ultimate competition men engage in" (p. 107). [*As many feminists have pointed out, this book is pretty sexist.*]

HARDING, SUSAN.
   "Women and Words in a Spanish Village." In Rayna Reiter, ed., *Towards an Anthropology of Women*. New York: Monthly Review Press, 1975.

An ethnographic account of the verbal role of women in the village of Oroel in northeastern Spain, this paper indicates a division of verbal skills, topics, and genres of speech that follows the division of labor between men and women. Women's verbal specialties center around home and family: the talk that accompanies childrearing; "intuition"—a special kind of empathy, an engagement with the needs and concerns of others; worry about the well-being of others; verbal finesse at penetrating the secrecy of men (secrecy that goes with the greater power and resources of males); chatting; story-telling; and gossip. "The skills and genres are essential to, integrated with, or extensions of the tasks and obligations of women as wives and mothers. However, women also use their verbal acts to reach beyond the official limits of their role in response to their subordinate economic and political position in the society. Whatever power and influence women have in the daily affairs of Oroel depends on how well they can wield words in certain ways. Yet each of the verbal skills has a double edge. At the same time it reflects a woman's effort to reach beyond her subordinate position in the village society, it returns and keeps her in that position." [*See IV-C, IV-F.*]

HEILBRUN, CAROLYN G.
   Toward a Recognition of Androgyny. New York: Alfred A. Knopf, 1973.

In discussing the advantages of androgyny—"a condition under which the characteristics of the sexes, and the human impulses expressed by men and women, are not rigidly assigned"—Heilbrun quotes from a commentary by J. B. Priestley ("Journey Down the Rainbow," *Saturday Review*, Aug. 18, 1956, p. 35) on life between the sexes in Dallas, Texas: "I am convinced that good talk cannot flourish where there is a wide gulf between the sexes, where the men are altogether too masculine, too hearty and bluff and booming, where the women are too feminine, at once both too arch and too anxious. Where men are leavened by a feminine element, where women are not without some tempering by the masculine spirit, there is a chance of good talk. And if there cannot be a balance of the two eternal principles, then let the feminine principle have the domination. But here was a society entirely dominated by the masculine principle."

HIRSCHMAN, LYNETTE.
    "Female-Male Differences in Conversational Interaction." Paper presented at Linguistic Society of America, Dec., 1973.

The females in Hirschman's analysis, in conversation together, interrupted or overlapped each other more than the male or mixed-sex pairs. Though they used a much higher percentage of fillers than did males overall, females showed their lowest percentage in conversation together, suggesting that they may be more at ease (more fluent, less hesitant) with a female than with a male. A "flow of conversation" analysis gave the impression that females talking to each other would elaborate on the other's utterance, while the males would dispute or ignore it. In mixed-sex dyads, a female-question/male-answer pattern emerged in several conversations. Hirschman found individual styles which *might* be gender-associated, e.g., one female used qualifiers of the type *I think, I'd say, I guess,* while a male used qualifiers of the type *most people, many females,* etc. Another style difference: one female made many false starts, repeated words as a hesitation device, left many sentences unfinished, and didn't leave many long pauses unfilled; both males generally finished the sentences they started, but often had long internal pauses in their utterances. Hirschman regards these as suggestive findings to be further investigated. [*See II-B, IV-A, IV-D, IV-E.*]

KEENAN, ELINOR.
    "Norm-Makers, Norm-Breakers: Uses of Speech by Men and Women in a Malagasy Community." In J. F. Sherzer and R. Baumann, eds., *Explorations in the Ethnography of Speaking.* New York: Cambridge Univ. Press, in press.

In the Merina tribe in Madagascar, strong value is placed on speaking indirectly and avoiding open confrontation. Men are regarded as skillful at this type of speech; they use an illusive and formal style. Women are seen as norm-breakers; they are associated with a direct, straightforward, impolite manner of speech, blurting out what they mean and communicating anger and negative information. Women are associated with bargaining, haggling, reprimanding children, and gossiping about shameful behavior. Men dominate situations where indirectness is desirable, such as ceremonial speech situations and inter-village relations.

KRAMER, CHERIS.
    "Folklinguistics." *Psychology Today,* 8 (June, 1974), 82-85.

According to popular belief (but not carefully controlled research), the speech of women is "emotional, vague, euphemistic, sweetly proper, mindless, endless"; in general it is supposed to be weaker, less effective, and more restricted than the speech of men. Kramer found such stereotypes reflected in *New Yorker* cartoons: women characters speak less, and in fewer places; when not shown in the home (where women are most often pictured), women often seem incapable of handling the language of the location, and their speech is the focus of humor. In general, women in the cartoons speak less forcefully than men, uttering fewer exclamations. Males use exclamations when they are angry or exasperated; women, more to convey enthusiasm. Male characters swear more freely than female characters. Kramer emphasizes that the stereotypes may not be true of actual speech, and reports an experiment which turned up no sex differences in choice of words. She also notes, "words, phrases, and sentence patterns are not inherently strong or weak. They acquire these attributes only in a particular cultural context. If our society views female speech as inferior, it is because of the subordinate role assigned to women. Our culture is biased to interpret sex differences in favor of men." [*See II-B, IV-D, IV-F.*]

ROSENFELD, HOWARD M.
"Approval-Seeking and Approval-Inducing Functions of Verbal and Nonverbal Responses in the Dyad." *Journal of Personality and Social Psychology*, 4 (1966), 597-605.

Rosenfeld experimentally constructed an approval-seeking condition for 13 male and 13 female dyads, and an approval-avoiding condition for 11 pairs of males and 9 pairs of females, by secretly instructing one member of each dyad either to gain or to avoid the approval of the other member. He examined verbal and nonverbal responses (gestures, speeches, utterances, and words) as they varied in each condition. In general, women used shorter utterances than men, especially in the approval-avoiding condition, and a greater proportion of their utterances consisted in answers to questions than did the utterances of men.

SOSKIN, WILLIAM F. AND VERA P. JOHN.
"The Study of Spontaneous Talk." In Roger Barker, ed., *The Stream of Behavior.* New York: Appleton-Century-Crofts, 1963.

To study spontaneous talking behavior in natural settings, the authors used miniature radio transmitters worn by a husband and wife at a large summer resort. The talk of the couple (Roz and Jock) during a 16-hour day was analyzed into episodes and phases; quantity of talk; frequency of different message types and functions (e.g. informational functions—factual statements about oneself and one's world, vs. relational functions—the range of verbal acts by which a speaker manages his interpersonal relations). In terms of message types, Roz (the wife) produced more affect-discharging messages; Jock (the husband), more directive and informational statements. When the two were in private, Roz produced more expressive messages than when they were in the presence of others. While Jock's conversation followed a single theme for some time, Roz on a number of occasions seemed to be trying to shift the conversation to other topics. In one episode, Roz and Jock were rowing and nearly capsized; Jock's dominant position was reflected in the low percentage of questions he asked (he mainly gave regulative statements—demands, suggestions, prohibitions—which "functioned to enhance his ego, control his environment, and allay anxiety"). Roz gave more descriptions of her present physical or psychological state; at the peak of the crisis, she made many requests for information; when the crisis passed, she expressed more delayed affect. In interacting with larger groups, Roz was more sensitive than Jock to her own impact on the group and to the possible interests and needs of other group members; she frequently acted as a "governor" for Jock, attenuating his impact on the group. Jock used a disproportionate amount of available talking time, and produced longer units of speech. The greatest similarity between husband and wife appeared in social settings calling for heavy reliance on informational language, and the greatest difference in social contexts of more intimacy where much of their talk consisted of relational language. [See IV-D, IV-G.]

STRODTBECK, FRED L. AND RICHARD D. MANN.
   "Sex Role Differentiation in Jury Deliberations." Sociometry, 19 (1956), 3-11.

Mock jury deliberations were recorded in a laboratory situation, with participants drawn from regular jury pools of Chicago and St. Louis courts. Analyzing the interaction of the jurors, the authors claim to have found a sex-role differentiation similar to that Bales and others have suggested for adults in the family: males played an instrumental, and females, an expressive (social-emotional) role. "Men *pro-act*, that is, they initiate relatively long bursts of acts directed at the solution of the task problem, and women tend more to *react* to the contributions of others." Almost twice as much of the women's talk consisted of agreeing, concurring, complying, understanding, and passively accepting; and less than half as much of the women's talk showed antagonism or deflated the status of others. [See IV-D.]

C. Speech Genres

In a given social group, there may be specific types of speech events, genres, rituals, or games particular to either sex. For example, in Turkey there is a form of *verbal dueling* unique to groups of teenage boys, involving homosexual content and a specific sequence and rhyme form (Alan Dundes, Jerry W. Leach, and Bora Ozkok, "The Strategy of Turkish Boys' Verbal Dueling Rhymes," in John J. Gumperz and Dell Hymes, eds., *Directions in Sociolinguistics* [New York: Holt, Rinehart & Winston, 1972], 130-160). Verbal dueling among black speakers in urban areas ("the dozens"; "sounding"; "signifying") may involve distinctions according to the sex of speakers and audience. Most studies of these speech forms have been based primarily on male informants (e.g., Roger Abrahams, *Deep Down in the Jungle*, revised edition [Chicago: Aldine, 1970]; Thomas Kochman, " 'Rapping' in the Black Ghetto," *Trans-Action*, 6, 4[1969], 26-34; William Labov, "Rules for Ritual Insults," in David Sudnow, ed., *Studies in Social Interaction* [New York: Free Press, 1972], 120-169). An exception, which draws largely on female informants, is Claudia Mitchell-Kernan, "Signifying," in Alan Dundes, ed., *Mother Wit From the Laughing Barrel* (Englewood Cliffs., N.J.: Prentice-Hall, 1973), 310-328; and "Signifying and Marking: Two Afro-American Speech Acts," in Gumperz and Hymes *(op. cit.)*, 161-179. Mitchell-Kernan notes that the sex of informants is important since males are more likely to engage in verbal dueling. "This is not to say that no woman ever engages in such speech acts as *sounding* or *playing the dozens*, but when she does, they are typically not in the context of the speech event 'verbal dueling.' Because verbal dueling permits a great deal of license (not absolute in any sense), women cannot be suitably competitive because other social norms require more circumspection in their verbal behavior" (Mitchell-Kernan, 1973, p. 328).

Riddling is another speech event in which sex differences have been found. Among the Dusun, in Southeast Asia, women prefer riddles using archaic words or syllables, while men use the more simply metaphoric type (John W. Roberts, and Michael L. Forman, "Riddles: Expressive Models of Interrogation," in Gumperz and Hymes, *op. cit.*, 180-209). Other speech genres in which the sex of speakers, audience, and target may make a difference include *joking* (Rose Coser, "Laughter Among Colleagues," *see IV-B;* G. Legman, *Rationale of the Dirty Joke, see II-A-1*); *swearing* (Cheris Kramer, "Women's Speech; Separate But Unequal?" *see II-B;* J. Klein, "The Family in 'Traditional' Working-Class England," *see IV-F*); and *story-telling* (Barrie Thorne, "Women in the Draft Resistance Movement: A Case Study of Sex Roles and Social Movements," *see IV-F*). Susan Harding ("Women and Words in a Spanish Village," *see IV—B*) discusses story-telling, *chatting,* and *gossip* as speech genres associated with women.

Referring to the U.S., Nancy Faires Conklin ("Toward a Feminist Analysis of Linguistic Behavior," *see I*) notes that women's talk is often characterized as *gossiping,* an activity with low value; if women elevate themselves above gossip, they are said to carry out *conversation,* which is still regarded as a form of entertainment. In contrast, professional men are said to engage in *discussions, conferences, meetings;* their talk is described as "business-like" and "talking straight from the shoulder." Women who enter the public domain may take on this type of speech; otherwise they may not be taken seriously. Conklin urges women to "develop strategies for dealing with the new interactional situations presented by board room and locker room talk, either acquiring the style of speaking which is considered appropriate for these occasions or establishing their credentials as group members with women's own forms. They must recognize, legitimize, and creatively develop their own speech genres. Clearly the back-slapping joke will never be a female vehicle."

Vocal music genres may vary by sex. H. J. Ottenheimer ("Culture and Contact and Musical Style: Ethnomusicology in the Comoro Islands," *Ethnomusicology,* XIV [1970], 458-462) reports that on the Comoro Islands between Madagascar and Mozambique, there is a sexual division in musical styles. In call and response vocal music genres, the men emphasize the solo part and women, the chorus; choral singing among men is restricted to religious chant; women provide ululation for men's music in their role as spectators.

D. Amount of Speech

ARGYLE, MICHAEL, MANSUR LALLJEE, and MARK COOK.
     "The Effects of Visibility on Interaction in a Dyad." *Human Relations,* 21 (1968), 3-17.

An experimental study in which visibility was varied in a dyad, and measures of several factors, including speech production, were made. The authors found that in male-female pairs, males spoke more than females, and that when males were invisible, their amount of speech increased by an average of 40%, while females reduced their speech by a similar amount. [*See IV-E; IX-F.*]

BERNARD, JESSIE.
   The Sex Game. New York: Atheneum, 1972.

"Women in task-oriented groups of mixed-sex composition often have a hard time getting the floor. An informal survey of television panel discussion programs showed that men out-talked the women by a considerable margin, as indeed they do also in laboratory studies," (e.g. Strodtbeck, "Husband-Wife Interaction Over Revealed Differences," [*in this section*]). "Perhaps because their voices are less powerful, women have a harder time getting the attention of the group; and they are more likely to lose it by successful interruption from men. Unless someone in the group makes a special effort to give time to the women, they may sit for long periods contributing nothing" (pp. 145-146). [*See IV-B, IV-G.*]

BROWNELL, WINIFRED and DENNIS R. SMITH.
   "Communication Patterns, Sex, and Length of Verbalization in Speech of Four-Year-Old Children." *Speech Monographs*, 40 (1973), 310-316.

An experimental study of 79 four-year-old children (half of each sex) doing a verbal task. The independent variables were communication pattern (dyad; triad; role-playing triad; small group) and sex. The dependent variables were mean length of verbalization and mean length of verbalization minus repetitions. (The authors note that the variable, "amount of speech produced," has been measured in various ways: average total number of words produced, amount of speech in a sentence, time periods of speech, length of response, and mean number of words per pause. Individual rates of speaking, size of group, and aggressiveness affect these measures.) The findings: a greater amount of speech was elicited in the small group situation than in the dyad. "Females produced significantly more speech across all conditions than did males. This evidence confirms earlier reports of female linguistic superiority in samples of white, middle-class children." [*See VIII-B.*]

CHESLER, PHYLLIS.
   "Marriage and Psychotherapy." In the Radical Therapist Collective, eds., produced by Jerome Agel, *The Radical Therapist.* New York: Ballantine, 1971, pp. 175-180.

"Even control of a simple—but serious—conversation is usually impossible for most wives when several men, including their husbands, are present. The 'wife'—women talk to each other, or they listen silently while the men talk. Very rarely, if ever, do men listen silently to a group of women talking. Even if there are a number of women talking, and only one man present, he will question the women, perhaps patiently, perhaps not, but always in order to ultimately control the conversation, and always from a 'superior' position." [*See IV-G.*]

HILPERT, FRED, CHERIS KRAMER, and RUTH ANN CLARK.
   "Participants' Perceptions of Self and Partner in Mixed-Sex Dyads." *Central States Speech Journal,* Spring, 1975.

Fifty-seven pairs of mixed-sex dyads discussed a specified problem for ten minutes. After the discussion each participant completed a questionnaire indicating whether self or partner contributed more to feelings of trust and friendship, contributed to the decision, and talked more. Both women and men selected their partners slightly more frequently than themselves as the person who contributed more to feelings of trust and friendship. In perceptions of who contributed more to the decision, men selected their female partners as often as themselves; women chose their male partners far more frequently than they chose themselves. In response to questions about perceived amount of speech, "women selected the man as the one who talked more 72 percent of the time, whereas the men selected themselves 58 percent of the time. Analysis of the actual amount of time talked revealed that the man spoke more in 59 percent of the dyads." (Overall women had accurate perceptions of who spoke more in 78% of the dyads and men in 70%, but where women were incorrect, their errors tended to be systematic, designating the man as dominant speaker when in reality it was the woman.) Women apparently were not unhappy with this situation; they expressed as much satisfaction with the decision and with their influence on it as did the men.

HIRSCHMAN, LYNETTE.
"Analysis of Supportive and Assertive Behavior in Conversations." Paper presented at meeting of Linguistic Society of America, July, 1974.

Probing sex differences in conversational assertiveness and supportiveness, Hirschman had pairs of subjects discuss a question for ten minutes (there was a total of four single-sex and eight mixed-sex conversations). Amount of speech (or obtaining and holding the floor, measured by quantity of speech, number of interruptions, and mean utterance length) was taken as one indication of assertiveness. It was hypothesized that men would be more assertive, and women more supportive in conversational behavior. No sex differences were found in amount of speech; "the number of conversations in which women talked more equalled the number of conversations in which men talked more. The average percentage of the word output was also equal for females and males." The differences in mean length of utterance were not statistically significant. In several cases the less coherent speakers had a high word output (taking more words to communicate one idea), but did not make a higher contribution to conversational content. [See II-B, IV-A, VIII-B.]

HIRSCHMAN, LYNETTE.
"Female-Male Differences in Conversational Interaction." Paper presented at Linguistic Society of America, Dec., 1973.

Hirschman found no clear gender differences in amount of speech, as measured by the length of time a person held the floor or the number of words produced, though informants were in the same order on the two measures. However, when the percent of time used for talking in a conversation (by either participant) was examined, it was found that more time was spent talking in conversations which had at least one female participant, suggesting that females may play a role in facilitating the flow of conversation. Referring to the style of her informant with the most floor time and word production, Hirschman suggests a possible female style, that "voluminous female speakers compensate for their possible aggressiveness by increased indications of hesitancy and increased responsiveness." [See II-B, IV-A, IV-B, IV-E.]

KENKEL, WILLIAM F.
"Observational Studies of Husband-Wife Interaction in Family Decision-Making." In Marvin Sussman, ed., *Sourcebook in Marriage and the Family*. Boston: Houghton Mifflin, 1963, pp. 144-156.

This is a laboratory study of two groups of 25 married couples at Iowa State Univ. The couples were young, well-educated, had at least one child, and the wife was a homemaker. Each couple was observed in a decision-making situation (deciding how to spend a sum of money); their behavior was analyzed using Bales' interaction process categories and other classifications. Among these couples, 52% of all husbands did most or more of the talking; the remaining 48% were divided between equal-talking couples and those where wives talked more (Kenkel doesn't give exact figures). Kenkel examined the relationship of amount of talk to influence ("influence" defined as "the degree to which a person is able to have his own wishes reflected in the decision of the group"). Among males, there was a tendency for high influence to be related to amount of talking. "For wives, the picture is less definite, partly because only four wives had a high degree of influence. There were, however, as many wives with medium influence as there were husbands. Among such wives only one did more of the talking; in most of the remaining cases, moreover, the husbands did the greater share of the talking. Apparently then, wives can actually achieve a medium degree of influence when their husbands do more of the talking or when the talking is distributed evenly. The reverse was untrue for husbands. Husbands had a two-to-one chance of achieving medium influence if they did the greater share of the talking; their chances were reduced to about one in three of influencing to this extent if the talking was distributed evenly; and in only one case did a husband achieve medium influence when his wife did more of the talking." Kenkel asked his subjects to rate who did the most talking; only "17 of the 50 individuals were able to judge accurately the distribution of the total amount of talking in their decision-making session."

KOMAROVSKY, MIRRA.
Blue-Collar Marriage. 1962; rpt. New York: Vintage, 1967.

In an intensive case study of 58 blue-collar couples, which included examining patterns of marital communication and power, Komarovsky found that, contrary to experimental findings with small groups, e.g., Strodtbeck, "Husband-Wife Interaction Over Revealed Differences," [*in this section*], amount of talk and dominance do not always go together. In several of the couples studied, the dominant partner was the less talkative of the two. "One can readily see that in a group of strangers a silent person can hardly make his influence count. In marriage, however, we deal not only with a smaller group but an enduring one. Over the years of marriage a person can exert his influence in other ways than through sheer volume of words. 'He doesn't say much but he means what he says and the children mind him,' a mother says about the father. The same may apply to the couple's marital relationship" (p. 353). [*See IV-F.*]

KRAMER, CHERIS.
"Folklinguistics." *Psychology Today,* 8 (June, 1974), 82-85.

Analysis of *New Yorker* cartoons revealed a "striking finding": women cartoon figures "did not speak in as many of the cartoons as did men" (a finding that goes against the popular stereotype that women talk too much). In the 156 cartoons in Kramer's sample, men speak 110 times, and women only 44. "In fact, the number of men goes up to 112 if we assume that a commanding voice from the clouds is that of a masculine God, and that a voice on the phone telling an elephant trainer to 'Give him two bottles of aspirin and call me in the morning' belongs to a male veterinarian." Kramer suggests several possible explanations for the relative silence of women: most cartoonists are men, and they may depict the people and activities they know best (male ones); men may try harder to be funny and make more comic statements; "or perhaps the cartoons reflect real life, where men like to have the last, topping word." [See II-B, IV-B, IV-F.]

KRAMER, CHERIS.
     "Stereotypes of Women's Speech: The Word From Cartoons." *Journal of Popular Culture*, in press.

This study of the speech of the sexes in cartoons in *The New Yorker, Ladies Home Journal, Playboy,* and *Cosmopolitan* does not confirm the claim that women's speech is "everlasting" (i.e., that women talk more than men). In the sample of *Playboy* cartoons, men talk 57 times, and women 32 times; in *New Yorker* cartoons men talk as much as two-and-a-half times more frequently than women; in *Ladies Home Journal* the caption is given to men as many times as to women (17 and 17); only in *Cosmopolitan* do women control more of the captions (11 men, 17 women). Females in the *Cosmopolitan* cartoons were more wordy than males (they had a higher average word count). Some of the length, Kramer suggests, "comes from an attempt on the part of women to soften the effect of their words." [See II-B.]

PARKER, ANGELE M.
     "Sex Differences in Classroom Intellectual Argumentation." Unpublished M.S. thesis, Pennsylvania State Univ., 1973.

Observations were made of 200 college students in discussion sections of introductory courses in history and sociology. Verbalizations were categorized by skill at intellectual argumentation. A questionnaire was administered, and subjects rated discussion behavior from "highly masculine" to "highly feminine" on a 4-point scale. Findings: males participated significantly more often than females, yet a greater number of females made at least one statement. Students rated intellectual participation behaviors as "masculine." The instructors participated significantly more frequently than the 200 students added together.

SOSKIN, WILLIAM F. AND VERA P. JOHN.
     "The Study of Spontaneous Talk." In Roger Barker, ed., *The Stream of Behavior*. New York: Appleton-Century-Crofts, 1963.

Studying the talk of a husband and wife at a summer resort (recorded by radio transmitters), the authors looked, among other things, at how much time each individual spent in talk (including variations in this amount by situation, activities, altered role relations). They found that the husband's claim on available talking time varied from 29% where he was having golf lessons, to 79% when talking with his wife. His total share of talking time across all situations was 50.6%. Not only did the husband talk more than the wife, but when the two were together, he produced longer units of speech. [See IV-B.]

STRODTBECK, FRED L.
"Husband-Wife Interaction Over Revealed Differences." *American Sociological Review,* 16 (1951), 468-473.

Strodtbeck had married couples fill out identical questionnaires as individuals and then, together, arrive at common answers for questions on which their initial responses disagreed. These discussions were taped and analyzed; two of the dimensions used were participation rates (amount of talk) and who "won" more of the contested decisions. Husbands talked more in 19 of the cases and wives in 15. For both husbands and wives, greater rate of talking was related to greater influence (winning more contested decisions).

STRODTBECK, FRED L., RITA M. JAMES and CHARLES HAWKINS.
"Social Status in Jury Deliberations." *American Sociological Review,* 22 (1957), 713-719.

Exploring the relation of status differences in the larger community to power and participation in face-to-face situations, the authors conducted mock jury deliberations with participants drawn by lot from the regular jury pools of Chicago and St. Louis courts (the jurors listened to a recorded trial, deliberated, and returned their verdict; 49 deliberations were recorded and analyzed, with 588 different jurors involved). Analysis of interaction showed that "men, in contrast with women, and persons of higher in contrast with lower status occupations have higher participation, influence, satisfaction and perceived competence for the jury task" (p. 718). Speaking time was distributed accordingly: in all occupational levels, males talked more than females.

STRODTBECK, FRED L. and RICHARD D. MANN.
"Sex Role Differentiation in Jury Deliberations." *Sociometry,* 19 (1956), 3-11.

In a study of the interaction of jurors involved in mock jury deliberations, the authors found that although men constituted about two-thirds of the juries studied, they contributed almost four-fifths of the talk. [*See IV-B.*]

SWACKER, MARJORIE.
"The Sex of the Speaker as a Sociolinguistic Variable." In Barrie Thorne and Nancy Henley, eds., *Language and Sex: Difference and Dominance.* Rowley, Mass.: Newbury House, 1975.

Thirty-four informants (17 men and 17 women) were separately shown three pictures by Albrecht Dürer and asked to describe what they saw, taking as much time as needed for their descriptions. Men were more verbose than women. The female mean time for all three descriptions was 3.17 minutes, and for males was 13.0 minutes; there were no significant sex differences in the speed of the discourse (words per minute). "These statistics are not entirely accurate because there were three male informants who simply talked until the tape ran out." Their times were arbitrarily set at 30 minutes for statistical purposes; even without "these exceptionally verbose males, the mean for men was significantly longer than that for females." [See II-B, IV-G.]

WOOD, MARION M.
    "The Influence of Sex and Knowledge of Communication Effectiveness on Spontaneous Speech." *Word,* 22, No. 1-2-3 (1966), 112-137.

An experimental study varying sex of speaker (18 subjects of each sex were individually tested); stimuli evoking spontaneous speech (speakers were asked to describe photographs of the same person with different facial expressions); sex of person spoken to; and knowledge of communication effectiveness (subjects were given different sets of "pseudofeedback" about success and failure). Interaction between speaker and hearer was limited to speech by the speaker (i.e., it was one-way with no nonverbal communication). It was found that: (1) "men tend to use more words per utterance in a given verbal task than do women"; and (2) "the length of the verbal output of males, but not of females, tends to increase under conditions of ineffective communication and to level off under conditions of successful communication." Wood suggests that "males are more sensitive to success or failure of communication than are females," and that "males may have a greater tendency to repeat" (related to their greater verbal output). [See II-B.]

E. Interruption

ARGYLE, MICHAEL, MANSUR LALLJEE, and MARK COOK.
    "The Effects of Visibility on Interaction in a Dyad." *Human Relations,* 21 (1968), 3-17.

An experimental study in which visibility was varied in a dyad, and speech patterns, among other things, were analyzed. The authors report that in an attempt to dominate, males interrupted more than did females (no figures are provided about this finding). [See IV-D; IX-F.]

HENNESSEE, JUDITH and JOAN NICHOLSON.
    "NOW Says: TV Commercials Insult Women." *New York Times Magazine,* May 28, 1972, 12+.

The New York branch of the National Organization for Women studied 1,241 television commercials. Almost all showed women inside the home doing household tasks or as domestic adjuncts to men. The commercials assume male authority; women never tell men what to do, but men continually give women advice and orders. The study found that 89.3% of the voice-overs are male (i.e., a woman may be the main figure in the ad, but her voice is followed by a male voice-over, the voice of authority, conferring the stamp of approval on the product). [*Voice-overs can be analyzed as a kind of interruption pattern.*]

HIRSCHMAN, LYNETTE.
"Female-Male Differences in Conversational Interaction." Paper presented at Linguistic Society of America, Dec., 1973.

Analyzing a small sample of dyadic conversations, Hirschman found that the female pair interrupted each other with a much higher frequency than the four mixed-sex pairs or the male pair. She suggests that her interruption measure may need to be refined, however, to exclude overlapping that occurs when one speaker anticipates the end of the other speaker's utterance, rather than is attempting to gain the floor. Such a measure would require "a much more sophisticated understanding of the set of cues used to signal the end of an utterance." [See II-B, IV-A, IV-B, IV-D.]

ZIMMERMAN, DON H. and CANDACE WEST.
"Sex Roles, Interruptions and Silences in Conversation." In Barrie Thorne and Nancy Henley, eds., Language and Sex: Difference and Dominance. Rowley, Mass.: Newbury House, 1975.

This paper is based on Harvey Sacks' work on rules governing the organization of conversation, e.g., rules that only one party speaks at a time, and that speaker change recurs. Related to this is the notion of a speaker's turn (bounded rights to speak, which may be violated by interruptions and speaking out of turn), and mechanisms for transition between speaker turns. Zimmerman and West examined transcripts of brief, two-party conversations, covertly recorded in public places. There were 11 male-female, 10 female-female, and 10 male-male pairs, all white, middle-class, from 20-35 years old, with relationships ranging from close friendship to casual acquaintanceship. The authors examined transcripts for instances of simultaneous speech—overlaps (where the current speaker has reached a point in her utterance that can be treated as a complete sentence and a non-speaker begins to talk while the current speaker continues; the speaker might protest, "I wasn't quite finished"); and interruptions (a non-speaker begins to talk at a point in the current speaker's utterance which cannot be viewed as a possible sentence completion point; the protest here would be, "You interrupted me"). In the single-sex conversations, which were combined for analysis, there were 7 interruptions and 22 overlaps, both symmetrically distributed between speakers. In male-female conversations there were 48 interruptions and 9 overlaps, which showed a dramatic asymmetric pattern: "virtually all the interruptions and overlaps are by the male speakers (98% and 100% respectively)." In no case did the woman who was interrupted protest. While in same-sex conversations the distribution of silence was nearly equal, in cross-sex conversations females showed more silence than males; women tended to fall silent for noticeable periods of time after being interrupted. Retarded minimal responses (e.g., "mm" or "um hmm") and interruptions—both more prevalent in the speech of males in cross-sex conversations—function as mechanisms to control the topic. This is reminiscent of adult-child conversations where the child, like women in these cross-sex conversations, has restricted rights to speak and to be listened to. The authors conclude that male dominance encompasses "routine chit-chat," since the woman's right to complete a speaking turn was routinely infringed upon without apparent consequence. [See IV-G.]

F. Conversational Topics

BARRON, N.M. and M.J. MARLIN.
"Sex of the Speaker and the Grammatical Case and Gender of Referenced Persons."
Technical Report No. CI 53, Center for Research in Social Behavior. Columbia: Univ.
of Missouri.

Videotapes of teachers and pupils in 6th and 11th grade classrooms were recorded,
reconstructed, and coded for a number of interpersonal and linguistic characteristics.
Analysis of the language of the teachers indicated, among other things, that both male and
female teachers talked about men more than about women. "It is presently a man's world in
the classroom despite its predominantly female population. The effects of this bias toward
the dominant masculine subcultures are yet to be documented, and then perhaps changed."

HARDING, SUSAN.
"Women and Words in a Spanish Village." In Rayna Reiter, ed., *Towards an
Anthropology of Women.* New York: Monthly Review Press, 1975.

In the village of Oroel in northeastern Spain, differences in conversational topics parallel
the division of labor between the sexes: men (whose domain is work in agriculture,
livestock, and in some shops and trades) talk of the land, crops, weather, prices, wages,
inheritance, work animals, and machinery. "On the side they may discuss hunting, play
cards, quote facts and figures of all sorts and argue about sports." The primary work of
women is at home; their talk is "wrapped around people and their personal lives," and the
needs and concerns of household members. [*See IV-B, IV-C.*]

KLEIN, J.
"The Family in 'Traditional' Working-Class England." In Michael Anderson, ed.,
Sociology of the Family. Baltimore, Md.: Penguin, 1971, pp. 70-77. Excerpted from
J. Klein, *Samples from English Culture,* Vol. 1. London: Routledge & Kegan Paul,
1965, pp. 103-113.

Within the culture of miners, there is strong segregation between the sexes. The woman's
place is in the home; the man's place is outside it, in his world of work, and with male
friends at the club, the pub, the corner, the sports-ground. "It is with other men that they
are at their most relaxed, at ease and emotionally expansive"; the bond between men is so
deep that in some ways they form a secret society, deliberately excluding women, children,
and strangers, partly through "pit-talk" or swear-words used familiarly within the group,
and offensively to those outside. "Women are not supposed to hear these words from men,
though they may use them in their own women's circle. Thus for instance the bookie's
office is part of the men's world, where women have no place. A woman going into the
office is subjected to jokes and language which in a more neutral locality would lead to a
fight." "Just as men in the clubs talk mainly about their work and secondly about sport and
never about their homes and families, so do their wives talk first of all about *their* work, i.e.

their homes and families, and secondly within the range of things with which they are all immediately familiar. The men discourage any transgressions over the line of this division of interests. When a woman does express any interest in politics or other general topics, she speaks rather apologetically, and can be prepared for her husband to tell her not to interrupt intelligent conversation: 'What the hell do you know about it?' " (p. 73). [See IV-C.]

KOMAROVSKY, MIRRA.
   Blue-Collar Marriage. 1962; rpt. New York: Vintage, 1967.

This is an intensive case study of 58 blue-collar couples, based on interviews and covering topics like conjugal roles, the division of labor, patterns of interpersonal communication, marriage and power, kinship relations, social life, and leisure. Looking at communication patterns, Komarovsky found a strong pattern of sex segregation of activities, interests, and talk. Each sex felt it had little to say to the other, and even in social situations involving couples, the sexes split up to talk. The men felt their wives talked about gossip and "silly" matters ("dirty diapers stuff," one said); the men talked to their male friends about cars, sports, work, motorcycles, carpentry, local politics. The women (who were aware that men deprecated their conversations) talked to women friends about family and interpersonal matters. Women were more dissatisfied than men with their mates' patterns of marital communication; the women complained that their husbands didn't listen, didn't reveal their worries, and didn't talk enough in general. [See IV-D]

KRAMER, CHERIS.
   "Folklinguistics." *Psychology Today,* 8 (June, 1974), 82-85.

Kramer analyzed 156 *New Yorker* cartoons. Among her findings: women and men discuss different topics. "Men hold forth with authority on business, politics, legal matters, taxes, age, household expenses, electronic bugging, church collections, kissing, baseball, human relations, health, and—women's speech. Women discuss social life, books, food and drink, pornography, life's troubles, caring for a husband, social work, age, and life-style." Students read the cartoon captions and tried (quite successfully) to indicate the sex of the speaker; several of the students. said they considered all statements about economics, business, or jobs to be male. Men, wherever they happen to be, are pictured in control of language, while women, especially if they step over the topical boundary, often seem incapable of handling the language appropriate to the new location, and their speech is a source of humor. [See II-B, IV-B, IV-D.]

LANDIS, CARNEY.
   "National Differences in Conversations." *Journal of Abnormal and Social Psychology,* 21 (1927), 354-375.

Landis collected 200 fragments of conversation overheard in London on Oxford and Regent Streets during the late afternoon and early evening, noting the sex of the speaker and the person spoken to. As in the Columbus sample (M.H. Landis and H.E. Burtt [*annotated below*]), the man-to-man conversations were about business and money (35%), amusements or sports (16%), and other men (15%). Englishwomen talked to each other of other women (26%), of themselves (20%), and showed a tendency to converse on a greater variety of topics than the women in the American sample. There were contrasts with the American sample in conversation between the sexes: Englishmen talked to Englishwomen about women (20%), clothes (16%), and themselves (16%). Englishwomen talked to Englishmen about other women (24%), and about themselves (12%). This study, Landis concludes, shows "the Englishman when talking to a feminine companion adapts his conversation to her interests while American women adapt their conversation to the interests of their masculine companions."

LANDIS, M.H. and H.E. BURTT.
    "A Study of Conversations." *Journal of Comparative Psychology,* 4 (1924), 81-89.

Following a method similar to Moore's [*annotated below*], the authors "wore rubber heels and cultivated an unobtrusive manner," overhearing and recording 481 conversations in Columbus, Ohio, in a variety of settings (street cars, railroad and subway stations, on campus, at athletic events, parties, churches, restaurants, etc.). They noted the conversational topic, time, place, sex of partners involved, and estimated social status. In male-male conversations, the most frequent topics were business and money (49%), sports or amusements (15%), and other men (13%). Women talked to women about men (22%), clothing or decoration (19%), and other women (15%). Women talked of persons in 37% of the cases. In sexually mixed groups, men talked to women of amusement or sports (25%), money and business (19%), and themselves (23%). Women talked to men of amusement or sports (24%), clothing or decoration (17%), and themselves (17%).

LANGER, ELINOR.
    "The Women of the Telephone Company." *New York Review of Books,* 14 (March 12, 1970 and March 26, 1970). Reprinted by New England Free Press, 60 Union Sq., Somerville, Mass. 02143.

After three months working (and observing) as a Customer's Service Representative in the New York Telephone Co., Langer concluded that in her department, staffed mainly by women, religion and politics were avoided in conversation. "This is not characteristic of the men's departments of the company where political discussion is commonplace, and I believe the women think that such heavy topics are properly the domain of men: they are not about to let foolish 'politics' interfere with the commonsensical and harmonious adjustments they have made to their working lives."

MARSHALL, LORNA.
    "Sharing, Talking, and Giving: Relief of Social Tensions Among !Kung Bushmen." *Africa,* 31 (1961), 231-246. Excerpted in Joshua A. Fishman, ed., *Readings in the Sociology of Language.* The Hague: Mouton, 1970, pp. 179-184.

Marshall reports ethnographic observations of talk among a hunting-gathering group in the Nyae Nyae region of South West Africa. Talking keeps up open communication among the members of the band; it is an outlet for emotions and means of social control. People cluster in little groups during the day to talk, and at night, talk late by their fires. Food is the subject talked about most often. The men's talk is often about hunting: about people's past hunts, wondering where the game is at present, and planning next hunts with practicality. "Women (who, incidentally, do not talk as much as men) gave me the impression of talking more about who gave or did not give them food and their anxieties about not having food. They spoke to me about women who were remembered for being especially quick and able gatherers, but did not have pleasurable satisfaction in remembering their hot, monotonous, arduous days of digging and picking and trudging home with their heavy loads" (p. 181 in Fishman).

MOORE, H.T.
"Further Data Concerning Sex Differences." *Journal of Abnormal and Social Psychology,* 4 (1922), 81-89.

Moore walked down Broadway in New York City, overhearing and recording 174 fragments of conversation, and classifying them according to the sex of the interlocuters. He found that men in talking to men discussed money and business (48% of the fragments), amusements or sports (14%), and other men (13%). Women talking to women discussed men (44%), clothing or decoration (23%), and other women (16%). Men talked to women about amusements or sports (25%), and money and business (22%). Women talked to men about other men (22%), and other women (13%).

THORNE, BARRIE.
"Women in the Draft Resistance Movement: A Case Study of Sex Roles and Social Movements." *Sex Roles: A Journal of Research,* 1, No. 2 (1975).

In a participant-observation study of the draft resistance movement from 1968-1969, Thorne found that women participants were continually placed in a secondary and subordinate role. Risk-taking (breaking ties with the Selective Service System through turning in a draft card, refusing induction, etc.) was a central Resistance tactic, and a criterion for full acceptance within the movement. Women (who were not eligible for the draft) were largely barred from risk-taking and from the central dramatic arenas of the movement: confrontations with draft boards at hearings, with army officials at pre-induction physicals and induction refusals, with judges at arraignments and trials. These confrontations lived on in a rich repertoire of anecdotes, which belonged to men and not to women. In story-telling sessions (a central conversational activity within the movement), women tended to listen while the men performed. This is an example of a more general phenomenon: the prevalence of all-male activities involving risk, violence, and danger, which become a basis for later story-telling (with women pushed into a listening role)—e.g. sports, army experiences, sailing, mountain climbing, hunting, and cockfighting. Childbirth may be one sphere of risky experience (which makes for good stories) available to women, but not to men, although prepared childbirth opens this sphere to males, at least in an observer role. [*See IV-C.*]

G. Control of Topics

The study of how topics are raised, dropped, developed, changed, and diverted in conversations may indicate sex differences; this is part of the general issue of control of conversations (see Phyllis Chesler, "Marriage and Psychotherapy," *under IV-D*). Don H. Zimmerman and Candace West ("Sex Roles, Interruptions and Silences in Conversation," *see IV-E*) found that when a female tried to develop a topic in her turns at talk, the male made minimal response ("um, um hmm"), which, along with more frequent interruptions by males, functioned as a mechanism by which men controlled the topic in mixed-sex conversations. Jessie Bernard (*The Sex Game, see IV-A*) uses a tennis metaphor for this pattern of minimal response: one partner (often the female) supplies all the balls, with none being returned. In a study of the talk of a couple in naturalistic settings, William F. Soskin and Vera P. John ("The Study of Spontaneous Talk," *see IV-B*) found that the husband's conversation followed a single theme, while the wife tried to shift the conversation to other topics. Bernard cites research by Harold Feldman (*Development of the Husband-Wife Relationship* [Ithaca, N.Y.: Cornell Univ. Press, 1965]) indicating that, at least in his sample of married couples, the woman's initiative in starting conversations was not rewarded. Initiation of discussion by the wife was found to be negatively related to the amount of time spent talking with one another daily. "The less he talked, the more she tried to get him to talk; or, equally probable, the more she tried to get him to talk, the less likely he was to want to talk." In an experimental study in which subjects separately described pictures, Marjorie Swacker ("The Sex of Speaker as a Sociolinguistic Variable," *see II-B*) found sex differences in markers used for shifting topics: women used significantly more conjunctions, and men more interjections. (e.g., "OK").

V. WOMEN'S AND MEN'S LANGUAGES, DIALECTS, VARIETIES

There is a fairly old literature about male-female language distinctions in non-Western societies. Key (see I) notes that "around the turn of the century and for a while thereafter interest in 'women's languages' ran high—perhaps triggered by the exotic accounts brought back by travelers who reported this phenomenon in far off places" (p. 15). This topic overlaps with others in the bibliography, especially "Sex Differences in Word Choice, Syntactic Usage, and Language Style" (II-B) and "Conversational Topics" (IV-F). In a more general way it points to a taxonomical issue: do these variations constitute separate languages, dialects, or language varieties or styles? (For a discussion of these terms see Joshua A. Fishman, The Sociology of Language, *Rowley, Mass.: Newbury House, 1972, pp. 15-18; and Susan Ervin-Tripp, "On Sociolinguistic Rules: Alternation and Co-occurrence," in John J. Gumperz and Dell Hymes, eds.,* The Ethnography of Communication, *New York: Holt, Rinehart & Winston, 1972, pp. 213-250.) See also the discussion at the end of this section.*

BODINE, ANN.
"Sex Differentiation in Language." In Barrie Thorne and Nancy Henley, eds.,
Language and Sex: Difference and Dominance. Rowley, Mass.: Newbury House,
1975.

Bodine's comprehensive review of the cross-cultural literature on sex-based differentiation in language draws heavily from ethnographic studies of non-European societies, particularly Amerindian, but also including Bengali, Carib, Cham, Chukchee, Hebrew/Semitic,
Indo-European, Japanese and Thai. A table based on her classification scheme (sex
differentiation in (1) pronunciation, or any of several forms, (2) based on sex of speaker,
spoken to, speaker plus spoken to, or spoken about) lists which languages contain which
types of differentiation. She traces the history of the literature and notes tendencies, often
influenced by the linguists' European backgrounds, influencing their reports. In particular,
they failed to classify gender with other forms of sex-based differentiation, overstated and
exaggerated types of differentiation not occurring in their own languages, and made
presumptions that the language used by males was the basic language, and that used by
females a deviation (hence the prevalence of the term "women's language" over "men's
language"). [*See I, II-B.*]

CAPELL, A.
Studies in Socio-Linguistics. The Hague: Mouton, 1966.

In Chapter 7, "Language and Social Groupings," Capell discusses "group or social
dialects," which may be distinguished along the lines of sex, rank, profession and
occupation. He reviews cross-cultural literature (from North and South America, and Asia)
showing sex differences in morphology, lexicon, and phonetic use.

CHAMBERLAIN, ALEXANDER F.
"Women's Languages." *American Anthropologist,* 14 (1912), 579-581.

This article reviews theories offered to explain the existence of separate "women's
languages" among primitive peoples. Older theories accounted for women's language among
the Carib by speculating that women belonging to foreign tribes were saved and
incorporated by the Caribs when the male members were exterminated. This theory has
been refuted. Others have looked to social-economic factors, such as differentiation of
occupation and labor; also "religious and animistic concepts in woman's sphere of thought,"
and "the play-instinct, which often makes itself felt longer in woman."

CONKLIN, NANCY FAIRES.
"Perspectives on the Dialects of Women." Paper presented at American Dialect
Society meeting, 1973.

Conklin reviews some of the early literature (Chamberlain, Flannery, Sapir) on
systematic differences between men's and women's speech, with emphasis on the issue of
language change. "Numerous cases have been recorded in which languages have lost
male/female distinctions. When a language is dying due to influence from some other

language (as with native American languages and English), male/female differences are apparently among the earliest linguistic fine points to be omitted by nonperfect learners. In many reports the existence of male/female differences is known only from tales or other archaic forms. Sex distinctions such as those discussed here seem, even in languages in full use, to be quite vulnerable to loss or merger. In the cases of natural linguistic change and of language decay which have been reported, it is the male forms which become generalized to all speakers, not the female ones." [See II-A-2, IV-B.]

CONKLIN, NANCY FAIRES.
    "Toward a Feminist Analysis of Linguistic Behavior." *The University of Michigan Papers in Women's Studies,* 1 No. 1 (1974), 51-73.

    Under the general rubric of "sex-marking in languages," Conklin discusses the literature on "so-called women's speech" (noting that the only cases which have been studied extensively are those where women's and men's speech differ radically, so distinctions are hard to overlook, e.g., Yana, Carib, Koasati). In these studies, "the men's language is always taken as the norm, and the women's language as deviating from that norm." Where the sexes use diverse language forms, there must be "some strong social motivation for stratification along sex lines to counteract the natural integration processes which normally go along with language contacts." In Carib society, the sexes were socially separate in types of labor; the women lived together with small children, and the men in their own quarters. Hence, social stratification was reflected in linguistic stratification. There is evidence from several dying native American languages that as native culture is westernized, "the men's form of speech becomes generalized and is used by both sexes." [See I, II-A-2, II-B, IV-C, IV-D, VI.]

FARB, PETER.
    Word Play: What Happens When People Talk. New York: Alfred A. Knopf, 1973.

    Written in a lively style for a general audience, and reporting the sociolinguistic research of others, this book includes discussion of sex differences. On pp. 47-50, Farb reviews some of the literature on male/female differences in pronunciation, vocabulary, grammar, and use of speech, among the Chukchi, the Yana, the Vakinankaratra of Madagascar, the Chiquito Indians of Bolivia, the Japanese, and the Gros Ventre Indians of Montana. Farb suggests that sex differences in English were probably more marked in the past, when the social lives of the sexes were more separate (and women, in particular, were more insulated than they are now). Farb concludes that "sexual distinctions in speech arose as assertions of male superiority" (p. 49), and that "differences disappear as the social status of women becomes more nearly equal to that of men" (p. 50). [See II-A-1; II-B, III-A, III-B-2.]

FARLEY, ALISON.
    "Sexism and Racism: A Linguistic Comparison." Unpublished paper, 1972 (Berkeley, Calif.).

    Farley draws social and linguistic parallels between blacks and women: both are minorities, experiencing discrimination in employment and status; both have indulged in group hatred and rejection; both minorities are now beginning to realize and accept their group identities with enthusiasm and pride. These two minorities "have in turn created separate linguistic systems" (the dialect of blacks is more unique than that of women, since women have not been physically isolated from the dominant white male culture, in the way blacks have [the special situation of black women is not discussed]). The lack of real power of both minorities is mirrored in language use: female speech has a connotation of lack of seriousness and importance; blacks may be extra verbal as a compensation for lack of power and prestige. Both blacks and women have used games of verbal subterfuge (for women, flirting, playing dumb, buttering up, being cute) to gain control over their lives. The verbal style of blacks and of women are more linguistically complex than that of the standard white male (e.g., women have been constrained to be indirect; blacks have developed a fluent and lively "rapping" style). Linguistically, women have a distinctive lexicon in some domains ("the conversation of the beauty parlor, the bridge shop or the kitchen would leave most men at a loss"). There is a long lexicon of distinctively black terms. In grammar, there are a few characteristically female forms (e.g., tag questions; the polite subjunctive); black dialect has systematic grammatical and phonological variants. "The final question is whether minority groups such as blacks or women will be integrated into the dominant culture to such an extent that the linguistic differences will disappear or dwindle to inconsequence, or whether the groups will achieve and maintain social, economic and linguistic independence."

FLANNERY, REGINA.
    "Men's and Women's Speech in Gros Ventre." *International Journal of American Linguistics,* 12 (1946), 133-135.

    Studying the Gros Ventre of the Fort Belknap Reservation in Montana, Flannery noted differences in vocabulary and pronunciation in the speech of men and women. In addition, there are gestures in the sign language used only by women, and women and men have distinctive calls. The Gros Ventre are aware that the sexes "talk differently," though no one could formulate the difference. When telling a story, the old people could give the interjections proper to the sex of the character quoted, but did not make the appropriate variation in pronunciation. But apart from such contexts, it was said that if a woman used men's words she would be considered mannish, and a man using women's words would be considered effeminate.

FURFEY, PAUL HANLY.
    "Men's and Women's Language." *The American Catholic Sociological Review,* 5 (1944), 218-223.

    Like Jespersen, Furfey believes that the terms "men's language" and "women's language" imply more than the facts warrant, since "there is no instance known to the writer in which the men and women of the same tribe speak entirely distinct tongues. The sex distinctions which have been discovered involve, not the language as a whole, but certain specific features of the languages, such as phonetics, grammar, or vocabulary." Phonetic differences between men and women have been reported from the Chukchi (a Mongoloid tribe in Siberia), in the Bengali language in eastern India, and from the Eskimo of Baffin Land. Among the Chiquito of Bolivia there are two genders in the men's language, which are not found among women. Less extensive grammatical differences have been reported from various American Indian tribes (the Yuchi, Koasati, Cree, Hitchiti) and the Thai. Differences between the sexes in vocabulary have been reported from the Carib, and the Yana (in northern California). Furfey concludes "sex may affect linguistic forms in three ways; for such forms may be modified by (1) the sex of the speaker, (2) the sex of the person spoken to, and (3) the sex, real or conventional, of the person or thing spoken of" (p. 221). On the social significance of linguistic sex distinctions, there is evidence that "the distinctions in question are bound up with a masculine assertion of superiority" (e.g., among the Chiquito, men and supernatural beings were classed in one category; women, the lower animals, and inanimate objects in another).

HAAS, MARY R.
    "Men's and Women's Speech in Koasati." *Language*, 20 (1944), 142-149. Reprinted
    in Dell Hymes, ed., *Language in Culture and Society*. New York: Harper & Row,
    1964, pp. 228-232.

    In Koasati, a Muskogean language spoken in southwestern Louisiana, there are well-defined differences in the speech of men and women (involving indicative and imperative forms of verbal paradigms). Haas lays out rules governing these differences by setting up the forms used by women as basic and the male forms as derived from these (e.g., "if the women's form ends in a nasalized vowel, the men's form substitutes an *s* for the nasalization"). While this procedure is largely arbitrary, in a few instances "the speech of women is seen to be somewhat more archaic than that of men and to this extent it is possible to justify the procedure on historical grounds." Members of each sex are familiar with both types of speech, and can use either as the occasion demands (e.g., a man can use women's forms when telling a story about a woman character). At the present only middle-aged and elderly women use the women's forms; younger women have adopted men's speech. Other Muskogean languages at one time had similar differences, but they have largely disappeared. Haas summarizes other evidence of sex differences in speech: from the Yana, the Eskimo, the Carib, the Chukchee, the Thai.

HERTZLER, JOYCE O.
    A Sociology of Language. New York: Random House, 1965.

    Under "The Biosocial Categories and Groups" (pp. 318-321) Hertzler briefly summarizes some of the studies of segregation of language by sex groups "among primitive people" (the Caribs; in Madagascar; among the Guaycurus of Brazil; in Surinam; in Micronesia; among American Indian tribes; in Japan). He concludes that "major differentiations of language between the sexes of a society are rare. Contact between the sexes is so continuous and so extensive that sharp differences cannot long be maintained" (p. 319).

JESPERSEN, OTTO.
    "The Woman," Chapter XIII of *Language: Its Nature, Development and Origin*.
    London: Allen & Unwin, 1922, pp. 237-254.

    "There are tribes in which men and women are said to speak totally different languages, or at any rate, distinct dialects." For example, there are reports dating back to 1664 that among the Caribs of the Small Antilles, each sex has expressions which the other sex understands but never uses. However, these special words account for only about one tenth of the vocabulary, and the sexes share the same grammar; hence there are *not* really "two distinct languages in the proper sense of the word." Verbal taboos distinguish the sexes in various societies; e.g., among the Caribs, men on the war-path use words forbidden to women, and among the Zulu in Africa, a woman is not allowed to mention the name of her father-in-law and his brothers. There are grammatical differences between the sexes among the Chiquitos in Bolivia. Jespersen variously attributes these sex differences in language to the social separation of the sexes, to different activities and interests, and to differences of rank and male domination. [*See I, II-B, VI.*]

KRAUS, FLORA.
  "Die Frauensprache bei den primitiven Vokern." Imago (Leipzig), 10, 215 (1924), 296-313. Kraus, psychoanalyst in Vienna between the wars, read this paper on May 14, 1924 before the Wiener Psychanalytischen Vereinigung; its written form unfortunately remains untranslated from the German.

  Kraus's paper, concerned with women's language in primitive societies, is important for the data contained and the insights presented but is of particular interest to those concerned with the history of ideas within the area of sex specific speech. The paper is divided into three parts: a survey of data showing sex specific items in a number of languages, a review of numerous attempts put forth to explain how language varieties developed along sex lines, and Kraus's own psychoanalytical explanation for the phenomena. The data, lexical and phonological and morphological, are drawn from a number of sources; nearly all of it may also be found in Jespersen, Reik, and/or Furfey. The second part concisely presents almost all of the theories, past and present, on the reasons for origins of sex specific language patterns; Kraus provides historically, sociologically, psychologically and religiously based notions with copious examples and thorough documentation. The last and most innovative section, Kraus's psychoanalytic theory on the origin of women's language, attributes its origin to *turned tongue,* a term designating a set of verbal ploys which allows the speaker to secretly discuss the socially unacceptable without actually naming the item or concept under discussion. [*Annotation by Marjorie Swacker.*]

LAKOFF, ROBIN.
  "Language and Woman's Place." *Language in Society,* 2, No. 1 (1973), 45-79.

  Lakoff asserts that women have a special style of speaking (which avoids strong or forceful statements; uses indirect, "polite" means of expression; and is often associated with triviality). This contrasts with the more male or neutral style (associated with power, forcefulness, important matters). Women are socialized to the special style (and considered "unfeminine" if they don't use it), but are also punished for it (accused of being unable to speak precisely, to express themselves forcefully, or to take part in a serious discussion). Hence, a woman is caught in a bind: to be less than a woman (if she doesn't use the accepted style) or less than a person (which the style implies). A male is faced with no such dilemma; if he learns the language of his male peers, he is accepted both as a man and as a person. Adult males use woman's language less than vice versa; women may learn to switch to the neutral (male) form under appropriate situations (in class, talking to professors, at job interviews, etc.). This, in effect, makes women bilinguals; perhaps they never really master either language; it may take extra energy to shift languages appropriately. Lakoff asks if linguistic indecisiveness (trying to decide whether to use neutral or woman's language) is one reason why women may participate less than men in class discussions. [*See I, II-A-1, II-B, III-B-3, VII.*]

REIK, THEODOR.
    "Men and Women Speak Different Languages." *Psychoanalysis*, 2, No. 4 (1954),
    3-15.

This is a rambling, psychoanalytic article which notes that in a number of "primitive"
societies each sex has unique words and expressions never used by the other sex, and which
are surrounded by taboos. Interprets "primitive word avoidances" psychoanalytically: e.g.,
avoidances of names (as in societies where women are not to pronounce the names of their
fathers or brothers-in-law) as protection against the danger of having contact with forbidden
objects. Word taboos are also present in our "civilization," e.g., in cases where husband and
wife avoid addressing each other by name. In modern societies "women form a speech
community of their own," their talk, especially about sexual and bodily matters, being
"elusive and allusive," "indirect," and "delicate" (perhaps, Reik claims, because "speaking
means doing in words"). "Men may use certain feminine expressions when they imitate
women's talking or when they are making fun of women's way of expressing themselves."
Reik does not emphasize the reverse phenomenon: men's talk; women making fun of men,
though he does say that men may show consideration for "well-bred members of the other
sex" by avoiding coarse or vulgar expressions, e.g., a sailor who told his "lady physician"
about having "intimate union with a girl"; since the patient couldn't talk freely, Reik urged
the female psychiatrist to transfer him to a male physician. Reik notes sex differences in
topic and in adjectives (male: "a regular guy," "a good Joe," "paying through the nose,"
"hell," "damned," "it stinks" . . . female: "darling," "divine," "sweet," "adorable," and
emotional expressions like "I could just scream"; "I nearly fainted"; "I died laughing").

TRUDGILL, PETER.
    "Language and Sex." Chapter 4 of *Sociolinguistics: An Introduction*. Harmonds-
    worth, Middlesex, Eng.: Penguin, 1974.

This chapter surveys sex differences in Amerindian languages, Jespersen's explanations,
the Koasati examples, data from studies of phonology in Detroit, and data from South
African English, Norwich British English, and Norwegian. [*Annotation by the author.*]

ADDITIONAL REFERENCES

Blood, Doris. "Women's Speech Characteristics in Cham." *Asian Culture*, 3 (1962),
    139-143.
Bogoras, Waldemar. "Chukchee." In Franz Boas, ed., *Handbook of American Indian
    Languages*, BAE-B 40, Part 2 (1922). Washington: Smithsonian Institution, 631-903.
Bunzel, Ruth. "Zuni." In Franz Boas, ed., *Handbook of American Indian Languages*, BAE-B
    40, Part 3 (1933-1938). Washington: Smithsonian Institution, 385-515.
Chatterji, Suniti Kumar. "Bengali Phonetics." *Bulletin of the School of Oriental Studies*, 2,
    No. 1 (1962), 1-25.
Das, Sisir Kumar. "Forms of Address and Terms of Reference in Bengali." *Anthropological
    Linguistics*, 10, No. 4 (1968), 19-31.

Dixon, Roland and Alfred Kroeber. "The Native Languages of California." *American Anthropologist*, 5 (1903), 1-26.
Dorsey, James, and John Swanton. *A Dictionary of the Biloxi and Ofo Languages*, BAE-B47 (1912). Washington: Smithsonian Institution.
Frazer, James George. "A Suggestion as to the Origin of Gender in Language." *Fortnightly Review*, 73 (1900), 79-90.
Kroeber, Theodora. *Ishi in Two Worlds*. Berkeley: Univ. of California Press, 1961.
Sapir, Edward. "Male and Female Forms of Speech in Yana." In St. W. J. Teeuwen, ed., *Donum Natalicium Schrijnen* (1929). Reprinted in David C. Mandelbaum, ed., *Selected Writings of Edward Sapir: In Language, Culture and Personality*. Berkeley: Univ. of California Press, 1949, pp. 206-212.
Wagner, Gunter. "Yuchi." In Franz Boas, ed., *Handbook of American Indian Languages*, BAE-B 40, Part 3 (1933-1938). Washington: Smithsonian Institution, pp. 293-384.

Women's Language as Deviant or a Special Case?

Many of these writings suggest not that women and men have separate, parallel languages, but that there is a woman's language as distinct from "regular," "normal," or "neutral" language (which is presumably a basically male turf, into which women may venture, but sometimes at the risk of being considered "unfeminine"). This may partly reflect a sexist bias in description (taking male behavior as the normal, the basepoint, and female behavior as deviant or abnormal), a practice Bodine (above) so well illuminates. It may also reflect real differences of power: since men dominate positions of public power (economic, political, religious institutions), their language forms have more recognized authority and legitimacy than those of women. As Lakoff (above) notes, men's language is being pre-empted by women, but women's language is not being adopted by men—just as women are moving into men's jobs more than vice-versa, and women are adopting male clothing styles more than the reverse. In short, "the language of the favored group, the group that holds the power, along with its non-linguistic behavior, is generally adopted by the other group, not vice-versa" (Lakoff, p. 50). This trend, which is of long standing, illustrates a broader social phenomenon known as "imitating the oppressor." On the general issue of whether or not women have—and/or should develop—a culture independent from that of men, see Ann Battle-Sister, "Conjectures on the Female Culture Question," Journal of Marriage and the Family, 33 (1971), 411-420.

VI. MULTILINGUAL SITUATIONS

CONKLIN, NANCY FAIRES.
    "Toward a Feminist Analysis of Linguistic Behavior." *University of Michigan Papers in Women's Studies*, 1, No. 1 (1974), 51-73.

Bilingual situations often present barriers to women, especially where women follow men to the latter's places of work or to live with the husband's family. In immigrant situations, men working outside the home come into contact with the dominant language;

women, located in the home, are isolated from the community at large. Youth may learn the dominant language, isolating older women still further. Conklin refers to Ervin-Tripp's study of Japanese "war brides" on the West Coast, whose bilingualism involved conflicting sets of values (Susan Ervin-Tripp, "An Analysis of the Interaction of Language, Topic and Listener," *American Anthropologist*, 66, No. 6, Part 2 [1964], 86-102). [*See I, II-A-2, II-B, V.*]

DIEBOLD, A. RICHARD.
　　"Incipient Bilingualism." *Language*, 37 (1961), 97-112. Reprinted in Dell Hymes, ed., *Language in Culture and Society*. New York: Harper and Row, 1964, pp. 495-506.

　　In a peasant Indian village in Oaxaca, Mexico, the inhabitants speak Huave as a first language; Spanish is learned relatively late in life, if it is spoken at all (learning Spanish goes along with greater social contact with and participation in the national life). Diebold conducted a census of the village to ascertain who was monolingual, and who bilingual, and to what degree. 81% of the total were monolingual. With regard to sex, "bilingualism is predominantly a male skill, 80% of bilinguals of both the subordinate and coordinate groups being males." Sex is related to occupation; monolingual Huave speakers (proportionately more female than male) had less contact with the outside than subordinate and coordinate bilinguals (the latter made frequent marketing trips or actually lived outside the community for periods of time).

HANNERZ, ULF.
　　"Language Variation and Social Relationships." *Studia Linguistica*, 24 (1970), 128-151.

　　Hannerz discusses a bi-dialect situation: that of ghetto blacks who have their own dialect, in addition to using standard English. In this case women are often more skillful at speaking standard English than are men, partly, Hannerz suggests, because "ghetto mothers often seem to attach greater weight to the schooling of daughters than sons." The working patterns of ghetto women expose them more to standard English than do the jobs of men; women are often found in "service roles" (domestic helper, waitress, sales person) which give them an opportunity to listen to and to practice standard English. In contrast, many ghetto men are in manual labor occupations where there is less extensive communication in standard English.

HUGHES, EVERETT C.
　　"The Linguistic Division of Labor in Industrial and Urban Societies." *Georgetown University Monograph Series on Languages and Linguistics*, 23 (1970), 103-119. Reprinted in Joshua A. Fishman, ed., *Advances in the Sociology of Language II*. The Hague: Mouton, 1972, pp. 296-309.

　　Starting from the general assumption that "language encounters, hence bilingualism, are a function of social organization," Hughes describes the linguistic division of labor in Montreal, where French is spoken by the majority of the population, and English is spoken by a numerical, but economically dominant, minority. In the delivery of professional services (e.g., medicine, religion, education) there are two sets of institutions: one French-speaking, the other English. In industrial and commercial organizations, the top levels usually use English to communicate with themselves and with their peers in other organizations. In communicating information and instructions downward through the organization, at some point translation into French must occur, for at the middle and bottom ranks, personnel are nearly all French-speaking. White collar occupations in Montreal include the female bilingual private secretary, who provides liaison communication. "Usually of upper middle-class French family, she has taken the bilingual secretarial course offered by a certain convent. She has developed to a fine point the art of answering a phone call in the right language, French or English." The male bilingual executive assistant "has some of the liaison functions of the bilingual secretary, but he also deals with people lower in the ranks inside the organization" (p. 110).

JESPERSEN, OTTO.
   "The Woman," Chapter XIII of *Language: Its Nature, Development and Origin.*
   London: Allen & Unwin, 1922, pp. 237-254.

"Among German and Scandinavian immigrants to America the men mix much more with the English-speaking population, and therefore have better opportunities, and also more occasion, to learn English than their wives, who remain more within doors. It is exactly the same among the Basques, where the school, the military service and daily business relations contribute to the extinction of Basque in favor of French, and where these factors operate much more strongly on the male than on the female population: there are families in which the wife talks Basque, while the husband does not even understand Basque and does not allow his children to learn it ... Vilhelm Thomsen informs me that the old Livonian language, which is now nearly extinct, is kept up with the greatest fidelity by the women, while the men are abandoning it for Lettish. Albanian women, too, generally know only Albanian, while the men are more often bilingual." [*See I, II-B, V.*]

LEOPOLD, WERNER F.
   "The Decline of German Dialects." *Word,* 15 (1959), 130-153. Reprinted in Joshua
   A. Fishman, ed., *Readings in the Sociology of Language.* The Hague: Mouton, 1970,
   pp. 340-364.

In postwar Germany many population movements contributed to the demise of local dialects and the strengthening of colloquial standard German. Leopold reports a study by Otto Steiner comparing south and north German dialects; Steiner found that "boys use the local dialect far more commonly than girls, who prefer High German (standard German). In both regions, for both sexes, the share of High German is much larger in the cities than in the adjoining rural districts" (p. 359).

LIEBERSON, STANLEY.
  "Bilingualism in Montreal: A Demographic Analysis." *American Journal of Sociology,* 71 (1965), 10-25. Reprinted in Joshua A. Fishman, ed., *Advances in the Sociology of Language II.* The Hague: Mouton, 1971, pp. 231-254.

Based on Canadian census data, this article analyzes trends in language usage in Montreal from the 1920's to the 1960's. Over this time, although the French are far more bilingual than the English, the two populations have been in contact without the decline of either language. Children are generally raised as monolinguals who do not become bilingual until they leave the home context for school and/or work; hence the bilingualism of parents does not lead to loss of the mother tongue among the next generation. Sex differences in bilingualism enter into this process. Men in Montreal are more bilingual than women; hence "many of the bilingual members of each ethnic group are married to monolingual mates who share only the same mother tongue." This helps maintain the common mother tongue in the next generation, since this is the one language both parents could use with the children. Lieberson compares male age cohorts with female age cohorts. The degree of bilingualism among girls under 15 is similar to that found for boys of the same ages (well under 1%). "Beginning with the late teens, at the age when formal education ends for many and participation in the labor force begins, we find increasing differences between the sexes in their bilingualism. By the early twenties, the sex differences in bilingualism are considerable." Women have a consistently lower increase in bilingualism, and they also show a net decline in bilingualism at an earlier age than men. Lieberson attributes these gender differences to "the influence of male participation in the labor force and female withdrawal into the home and child-rearing," contending that "the main supports of bilingualism are school and occupational systems."

RUBIN, JOAN.
  "Bilingual Usage in Paraguay." In Joshua A. Fishman, ed., *Readings in the Sociology of Language.* The Hague: Mouton, 1970, pp. 512-530.

Paraguay has a high degree of bilingualism; more than half of the population speaks both Guarani (an Indian language) and Spanish (which has generally higher social status than Guarani). Rubin used a questionnaire to probe social factors influencing choice of language among bilinguals. Among other things, she found sex to be a variable. Men whose first language was either Spanish, or both Guarani and Spanish, tended "to use more Guarani with other men, but to use Spanish with women who are their intimates. Women, on the other hand, whose first language was either Spanish or both, tend to use Spanish to both male and female intimates" (p. 528).

TABOURET-KELLER, ANDREE.
  "A Contribution to the Sociological Study of Language Maintenance and Language Shift." In Joshua A. Fishman, ed., *Advances in the Sociology of Language II.* The Hague: Mouton, 1971, pp. 365-376.

A study of the shift to Standard French from the regional *patois* in Pays D'Oc and from a German dialect in Alsace, based on data about the linguistic usage of children ages 7 to 15. The analysis stresses economic and migration patterns, but also mentions sex differences in use of the *patois*. In Pays D'Oc 28% of girls and 23% of boys in the sample speak the *patois* (the difference is not statistically significant). Children tend to speak *patois* more with their fathers (58.5%) than with their mothers (45.7%), a statistically significant difference; use of *patois* with the father increases from the age of 12 onwards.

Note on Black English and U.S. Minorities

This Bibliography, relying largely on middle-class white academic sources, reflects its middle-class white academic bias: there is little material available on sex differences in the language of blacks and other U.S. racial and ethnic minorities. The following papers, cited in this section and elsewhere in the Bibliography, will be helpful to those seeking information relevant to the intersection of race and sex with language:

III-A	Anshen, Wolfram
IV-B	Abrahams, Grier and Cobbs
IV-C	Abrahams, Kochman, Labov, Mitchell-Kernan
	(two references)
V	Farley
VI	Conklin (on Ervin-Tripp), Hannerz
VII	Stewart
IX-A, D, F	Johnson

VII. LANGUAGE ACQUISITION

[Note: For further reference on language acquisition, see also VIII, VERBAL ABILITY, since many of the papers cited there report studies of children.]

BERNSTEIN, BASIL, ed.
    Class, Codes and Control, II: Applied Studies Towards a Sociology of Language. Boston: Routledge & Kegan Paul, 1973.

This book, reporting sociolinguistic research of Basil Bernstein and his colleagues at the Sociological Research Unit of the University of London Institute of Education, reflects their concern with class differences in "maternal language" (the language spoken by mothers to children). Among the topics explored: maternal orientations to communication; different strategies mothers use in controlling their children; interrelations among sex, class, and hesitation phenomena.

CHERRY, LOUISE.
    "Teacher-Child Verbal Interaction: An Approach to the Study of Sex Differences." In Barrie Thorne and Nancy Henley, eds., *Language and Sex: Difference and Dominance.* Rowley, Mass.: Newbury House, 1975.

Cherry recorded spontaneously occurring conversations among four female preschool teachers and their 38 children (16F, 22M) in the Boston area; there were ten data samples from each teacher, and over 16 hours of recording. *All* vocalizations were transcribed by two assistants (1F, 1M), with high agreement, and children's names were coded on transcripts so that sex could not be known. Cherry analyzed verbal interactions with attention to *initiator* (of the interaction), speaker *turns, words, utterances, attentional markers, repetitions, directives,* and *question-answer verbal acknowledgement* sequences. Totals were analyzed and tested for significance by two-way analysis of variance. A hypothesis that teachers' verbal interactions with girls would be more fluent (more utterances and more turns per interaction) than with boys was not confirmed, nor was one that teacher-girl verbal interactions would be more likely than teacher-boy interactions to have been initiated by the teacher. Teachers verbally acknowledged a significantly greater percentage of teacher-girl question-answer sequences than teacher-boy ones, contrary to expectation. Teachers used more "controlling" speech—more attentional-marked and more directive utterances—to boys, though the latter finding was not statistically significant. [*See VIII-B.*]

GARCIA-ZAMOR, MARIE A.
    "Child Awareness of Sex Role Distinctions in Language Use," paper presented at Linguistic Society of America, Dec., 1973. (Garcia-Zamor is at International Bank for Reconstruction and Development, Washington, D.C.)

Eight nursery school children, four boys and four girls 5½-6 years old (middle and upper middle class), were interviewed twice: first, with a questionnaire designed to elicit overt attitudes toward sex roles: second, in a situation designed to determine how aware they are of "male" vs. "female" language. In the latter, the children gave judgments about whether a girl- or boy-doll prop uttered sentences containing terms of endearment, hostility, aggression, color terminology, elevating and derogatory terms, automotive terms, expressions of thoughtfulness, and tag questions. In the first interviews, traditional notions about sex roles were exhibited, with girls voicing far more of these views than boys, despite the fact that the nursery school is one that consciously attempts to combat sexism. Specifically, the girls had already begun to define themselves and females in general as inferior to males, and to circumscribe a limited range of life choices for themselves based on sex. In the language study, there was more agreement among the male subjects than among the females about whether an item was uttered by a male or female; and most of their instances of agreement were around terms ascribed to the male doll. The results are somewhat complex, and the following serves as only a suggestive summary of the findings: "Aggressive" (and competitive) expressions were consistently associated with the male doll; *"Dum-dum"* (devaluative) combined with accidental breaking was female-associated. Bright colors describing clothing were male-associated, light ones female-associated. Cars were more associated with males than females, across the automotive-term and color sentences. Tag questions tended to be female-associated. Judgments for terms of endearment and for epithets were mixed, though *shit* was seen by both boys and girls as male, and *drat* was seen by both as female; *daddy* was seen by both as male. Garcia-Zamor sees these results as "pointing to the durability of sex-based attitudes" and suggesting that "at this age boys make more consistent judgments about the appropriateness of language use on the basis of sex than girls do," though the girls had stronger sex-biased notions than the boys. She suggests that "it is the boys who are currently learning a new language—male language . . .

With his heightened level of linguistic sophistication the child can now differentiate between woman's language, his pre-school language, and the language of the male with whom he prefers to identify . . . The girls . . . merely continue in the language of the nursery. The only aspects of male language they need learn are those proscribed to them (for example, strong epithets), which this study shows they do learn." [*See II-B.*]

GLEASON, JEAN BERKO.
"Code Switching in Children's Language." In Timothy E. Moore, ed., *Cognitive Development and the Acquisition of Language,* pp. 159-167. New York: Academic Press, 1973.

This paper reports an observational study of the child's emerging control of different language styles, made on natural conversations in families with several children, ranging in age from infancy to eight years. In adult-to-child communication, distinctions were found between the manners of address to boy and girl children. Boy babies might be addressed in a "Hail-Baby-Well-Met style," especially by fathers, while being played with heartily. "Girl babies were dealt with more gently, both physically and verbally." A sex difference is mentioned in children's own language, in the sound effects accompanying play: though the actual differences aren't described, "the boys played more violent games and accompanied them with appropriate sound, but the girls made a lot of noises as well."

LABOV, WILLIAM.
Sociolinguistic Patterns. Philadelphia: Univ. of Pennsylvania Press, 1972, pp. 243, 301-304.

In terms of phonology, women are more sensitive to prestige patterns, and often use the most advanced forms in their own casual speech. Hence women play an important part in the mechanism of linguistic change. "To the extent that parents influence children's early language, women do so even more; certainly women talk to young children more than men do, and have a more direct influence during the years when children are forming linguistic rules with the greatest speed and efficiency. It seems likely that the rate of advance and direction of a linguistic change owes a great deal to the special sensitivity of women to the whole process" (p. 303). [*See III-A.*]

LAKOFF, ROBIN.
"Language and Woman's Place." *Language in Society,* 2, No. 1 (1973), 45-79.

Children are ostracized, scolded, or made fun of by adults and peers for not speaking the correct language for their sex. But if the little girl learns her lesson well, her "women's language" will later be an excuse others use to keep her in a demeaning position and to refuse to take her seriously. In a long footnote Lakoff amplifies on children's learning of sex-differentiated language. Probably both boys and girls first learn "women's language" (in Japanese, both sexes start out with particles proper for women, but boys are ridiculed if they speak them after about 5 years). As they mature, boys go through a stage of rough talk, which is discouraged in girls; at around 10, when they split up into same-sex peer groups, the two languages seem to be present. Boys have unlearned their original language and adopted new forms, while girls retain their old speech. Most of the phonological, syntactic, and semantic structure of language is in active use by 4 or 5, but social-contextual factors are not put into use until much later. Note that children have not learned the rules of polite conversation and blurt out inappropriate remarks. Lakoff suggests research in the acquisition of rules of contextual appropriateness, perhaps more accessible to research than syntactic and semantic acquisition. In suggesting that women who want to be taken seriously, who enter the public domain (professions, classrooms, etc.), learn the more male or "neutral" forms, Lakoff points to another language learning (and unlearning) process. [*See I, II-A-1, II-B, III-B-3, V.*]

LEWIS, MICHAEL.
    "Parents and Children: Sex-Role Development." *School Review,* 80 (1972), 229-240.

Lewis reviews his own research and that of others regarding sex-role socialization, and points out that from before the child is born, its sex is the characteristic most attended and responded to. With regard to vocal interaction, he reports that "It has been found repeatedly that from the earliest age mothers look at and talk to their girl infants more than they do their boy infants. In fact, looking-at and talking-to behaviors are greater for girls over the entire first two years of life."

SACHS, JACQUELINE.
    "Cues to the Identification of Sex in Children's Speech." In Barrie Thorne and Nancy Henley, eds., *Language and Sex: Difference and Dominance.* Rowley, Mass.: Newbury House, 1975.

Prepubertal boys and girls can typically be identified as to sex from their voices. This paper presents three studies on the cues used in this identification. (1) Judges were able to guess the sex of the child from hearing isolated vowels, though not as well as from sentences. (2) Judges could not accurately determine sex from sentences played backwards, suggesting that, beyond the phonetic aspects of the voices, there is considerable information in normal sentences that carries information about the sex of the speaker. (3) When judges rated spoken sentences on semantic differential scales, a factor emerged that was correlated with the perceived masculinity or femininity of the voice, along with two other factors, Active-Passive and Fluent-Disfluent. This result suggests that there is an independent cue to the sex of the speaker that does not involve how active the voice sounds or how fluent it is. [*Author's annotation.*] [*See III-B-2.*]

SACHS, JACQUELINE, PHILIP LIEBERMAN, and DONNA ERICKSON.
    "Anatomical and Cultural Determinants of Male and Female Speech." In Roger W. Shuy and Ralph W. Fasold, eds., *Language Attitudes: Current Trends and Prospects.* Washington: Georgetown Univ. Press, 1973, pp. 74-84.

In our culture there are variations in speech style when adults speak to babies; some aspects of this speech style "may be an exaggeration of features that distinguish feminine from masculine speech, such as higher perceived pitch and variability in intonation. The situations in which people use this speech style have a feature in common—they are what

J. P. Scott [*Animal Behavior*, Chicago: Univ. of Chicago Press, 1958] has called care-giving, or 'epimeletic,' situations. Courting couples sometimes speak a type of 'baby-talk' and some people use it when talking to pets. The care-giving role in our culture is considered most appropriate for females, but both women and men typically are embarrassed about using baby-talk, or claim they don't use it." In Arabic, however, both men and women use a conventionalized baby-talk to babies, although it is considered more appropriate for women. [*See III-B-2.*]

STEWART, WILLIAM A.
   "Urban Negro Speech: Sociolinguistic Factors Affecting English Teaching." In Roger
   W. Shuy, ed., *Social Dialects and Language Learning.* Champaign, Ill.: National
   Council of Teachers of English, 1964, pp. 10-18.

This paper on teaching standard English to speakers of "radically nonstandard dialects" contains brief comments on the range of dialects spoken by blacks in Washington, D.C. The least standard dialect (which Stewart calls the *basilect*) is largely restricted to young children. At about the age of seven or eight, there is (at least for boys) a noticeable dialect shift (e.g., the acquisition of new grammatical morphemes) which "appears to take place quite automatically, and in fact seems fairly independent of formal education, although the change may be accelerated and linguistically affected by it" (p. 17). The change coincides with the shift males make at that age from the status of "small-boy" to "big-boy" in the informal social structure of the local peer group. "Since 'big-boys' seem to regard basilect as 'small-boy talk' (just as adults do), the continued use of pure basilect probably becomes undesirable for a boy who aspires to status in the older age group." (p. 17). Stewart adds in a footnote (which leads one to wonder if all of his previous comments were about males only) that this kind of rapid dialect shift is less frequent among lower class girls, because age-grading is much less rigid among them than among boys. In the case of girls, dialect change seems to be more a direct result of formal education.

VIII. VERBAL ABILITY

A. General

GARAI, JOSEF E., and AMRAM SCHEINFELD.
   "Sex Differences in Mental and Behavioral Traits." *Genetic Psychology Monographs,*
   77 (1968), 169-299.

Females have better fluency and facility with language than males, giving them superiority in literature, essay writing, spelling, grammar, and foreign language learning. Earlier maturation of the speech organs leads to earlier age of speech onset of girls. Girls have better articulation than boys, and all speech disturbances are more frequent among males of all ages. Girls' earlier speech development, greater fluency, and greater language consciousness are related to earlier maturation of their speech organs, "their innate tendency toward more sedentary pursuits," closer contact with mothers, greater interest in people, socialization to social responsiveness and compliance, and perhaps to genetic factors which produce more speech defects in boys. These findings and others more related to intelligence testing (e.g., "verbal reasoning") are discussed in relation to reasoning and intelligence, and their implications for vocational and social roles. [See VIII-B, VIII-C.]

McCARTHY, DOROTHEA.
   "Some Possible Explanations of Sex Differences in Language Development and Disorders." *Journal of Psychology*, 35 (1953), 155-160.

McCarthy claims small but important differences favoring girls over boys, in "practically all aspects of language development which show developmental trends with age" among white American children, from the age of onset of true language. [See VIII-C.]

THOMPSON, WAYNE N.
   Quantitative Research in Public Address and Communication. New York: Random House, 1967.

This volume summarizes and evaluates quantitative research on public speaking, drawing mainly on research published in speech journals, such as *Quarterly Journal of Speech* and *Journal of Communication.* For each topic the author lists studies, with brief annotations, and then draws conclusions (which often claim more than the studies support). There are sections reporting differences between the sexes as public speakers and as listeners (audience members). In the area of public speaking, the following sex differences have the most research support: Women speakers are superior in such uses of language as vocabulary, sentence structure, and grammar; they are also less fidgety and better integrated than male speakers. Men speakers are "less withdrawn, have greater confidence, are more animated, and have more useful physical activity" (p. 88). Thompson continues, "The one study indicating that verbal comprehension and reasoning were negligibly correlated with speaking effectiveness for women raises the interesting question: If female persuasiveness is not dependent on reasoning, what are its constituents?" (p. 88). Later, Thompson reports on sex differences in stage fright. Three studies found that male public speakers report more self-confidence and less fear than female public speakers. These were self-reports; judges, however, observed stage fright more in men than in women (e.g., the findings that men are more fidgety as public speakers). One study reported that men were more fidgety, unintegrated, and had poorer sentences and poorer articulation as public speakers. In another section, Thompson generalizes about the sexes as listeners: (1) As listeners, "women may be more persuasible than men"; "the range of topics and situations producing greater persuasibility for females is impressive, and in no study published in the speech literature were the men more impressionable" (pp. 45-46). (2) As listeners, women are "more responsive, perceptive, flexible, impressionable, and teachable than men" (p. 47). The studies cited include one that found that in learning a new language, boys were less able to make articulatory coordinations; another concluded that women were more accurate than men in identifying emotion portrayed nonverbally by two different instructors; a third found that women were more sensitive to nonverbal communication through tones. (3) "College men may retain more from an oral presentation than college women" (p. 48), based, for example, on a study comparing scores of men and women on a multiple choice retention test. Thompson acknowledges that the data are not clear-cut: there are 5 studies, with women scoring higher than men in one of them, and nonsignificant differences in 2. (4) "Men and women do not differ significantly in their responses to communication when the emotional involvement is minimal" (p. 49), based on 6 diverse studies (e.g., one finding that sex was not a factor in ratings of voice quality, personality, and teaching effectiveness;

another finding that the sexes did not differ in ability to choose the best reason in support of a conclusion). The author further concludes (without really clarifying the terms used); "The boundary between areas of significant and nonsignificant sex differences seems clear. In those matters in which perceptiveness, flexibility, and emotional responsiveness are of primary importance, a difference exists; in those requiring deliberate judgment, there is no difference" (p. 50). [*There is a literature, not included in this bibliography, on sex differences in persuasability of listeners, and on the credibility which audiences grant male vs. female speakers; this reference is a lead into some of that literature.*]

WINITZ, HARRIS.
    "Language Skills of Male and Female Kindergarten Children." *Journal of Speech and Hearing Research,* 2 (1959), 377-386.

    Although previous investigations have generally shown girls to be superior to boys on several language skills (Winitz cites 7 studies), the differences have been small and rarely significant, and other studies have contradicted the findings. A table summarizes the findings on 6 common measures, from 9 studies with a total of 124 tests: the differences favor girls almost two to one, though they are seldom significant (6 out of 7 significant differences favor girls, however). In many studies IQ and socioeconomic status have been uncontrolled and there are suggestions of boy-girl differences in them. Winitz's aim is to conduct language measures on equivalent and fairly large populations of boys and girls, to determine whether previous findings of female superiority are real or due to chance. The subjects were 75 girls and 75 boys—white, urban, nonstutterers of normal IQ and hearing—about to enter kindergarten in the Iowa City area, proportionately sampled from all kindergartens in the system. Measures of intelligence, socioeconomic status, and family constellation (older or younger siblings, both, or none) shows the two sex groups to be essentially equivalent on nonlanguage measures. On 6 measures of verbalization, elicited by stimulus pictures, girls were significantly superior in two (mean of longest responses, mean standard deviation); all differences in the other measures (response length, one-word responses, number of different words, structural complexity) also showed (nonsignificant) superior performance by girls. Girls were also significantly superior in one test of fluency, giving child names. On the other fluency measures (giving rhymes, adult names, and thing names) and on measures of articulation and vocabulary there were no significant differences, boys and girls showing superiority about equally. Winitz concludes that "the hypothesis of no language difference between the sexes is tenable in the population of five-year-old children with regard to major verbalization measures, articulatory skills, vocabulary skills, and three of four word-fluency measures." The differences in verbalization were not significant in the measures "generally regarded as of major importance," i.e., response length, structural complexity, and number of different words. "Female superiority in naming children may be the result of the tendency for girls to be more sociable than boys." He takes up but dismisses the possibility that a reason for not obtaining significant differences was that the examiner was male. [*Interestingly enough, the authors of all (8) studies cited as finding female superiority are female (one study had four female authors!). Of the two cited finding male superiority, one was co-authored by a male and female; the other was specifically mentioned as having used three male investigators out of ten.]* Child development has been primarily a women's field, and was especially so in the days of these studies.

B. Fluency

BROWNELL, WINIFRED, and DENNIS R. SMITH.
　　"Communication Patterns, Sex, and Length of Verbalization in Speech of Four-Year-Old Children." *Speech Monographs,* 40 (1973), 310-316.

This is an experimental study of 79 four-year-old children (half of each sex) in six Head Start centers. The children were shown objects and asked to name them, to indicate which of the objects go together, and to tell why. The independent variables were communication pattern (dyad; triad; role-playing triad; small group) and sex. The dependent variables were mean length of verbalization and mean length of verbalization minus repetitions. The findings: a greater amount of speech was elicited in the small group situation than in the dyad. "Females produced significantly more speech across all conditions than did males. This evidence confirms earlier reports of female linguistic superiority in samples of white, middle-class children." [*See IV-D.*]

CHERRY, LOUISE.
　　"Teacher-Child Verbal Interaction: An Approach to the Study of Sex Differences." In Barrie Thorne and Nancy Henley, eds., *Language and Sex: Difference and Dominance.* Rowley, Mass.: Newbury House, 1975.

A finding of superior verbal fluency in females has been reported as one of the most consistent and stable psychological sex differences to be found. Cherry examines the bases for this claim (with reference to preschool children), with a critique of the methodology and assumptions of the naturalistic observational studies cited, and reports her own research on teacher-child dyadic verbal interaction. Previous studies often transformed the raw data (e.g., omitting "meaningless vocalizations"), and depended on hand transcription, leaving the possibility that the observers' preconceptions biased their transcriptions. There has further been an assumption that verbal fluency is a characteristic of an individual speaker, whereas it is better conceptualized as a part of verbal interaction between two or more speakers. Cherry recorded spontaneously occurring conversations among four female preschool teachers and their 38 children (16 F, 22 M) in the Boston area and looked at, among other factors, fluency as an interactive variable. She failed to find greater fluency (measured either by utterances or by turns per interaction) in teacher-girl interactions than in teacher-boy ones. [*See VII.*]

GALL, MEREDITH D., AMOS K. HOBBY, and KENNETH H. CRAIK.
　　"Non-Linguistic Factors in Oral Language Productivity." *Perceptual and Motor Skills,* 29 (1969), 871-874.

This study provides evidence that women are more verbally fluent than men: "women attained a higher mean word count than men in eight of nine descriptions of verbal displays. On three of the comparisons, the sex differences are statistically significant." Correlating word count scores with personality variables as assessed by the California Psychological Inventory, the authors found that, for women, verbal fluency had a negative correlation with "good impression"; but for men, the correlation was consistently positive.

GARAI, JOSEF E., and AMRAM SCHEINFELD.
"Sex Differences in Mental and Behavioral Traits." *Genetic Psychology Monographs*, 77 (1968), 169-299.

Females have been reported to possess greater verbal fluency than males from infancy on. Earlier maturation of the speech organs leads to the widely observed earlier age of speech onset of girls. Girls have been observed to show greater verbal fluency from 12 months on with the beginning of articulate speech, throughout the preschool period, throughout elementary school, and in high school and college. From 18 months on, girls made fewer grammatical errors than boys; in sentence complexity, girls surpass boys at all ages from 18 months on, and were also ahead of boys in sentence length from 18 months. Girls have been reported to have better articulation than boys, and speech defects of all kinds are more prevalent in boys. [See VIII-A, VIII-C.]

HIRSCHMAN, LYNETTE.
"Analysis of Supportive and Assertive Behavior in Conversations." Paper presented at meeting of Linguistic Society of America, July, 1974.

Probing sex differences in conversational assertiveness and supportiveness, Hirschman had pairs of subjects discuss a question for ten minutes (the resulting conversations included four single-sex, and eight mixed-sex). It was assumed that fluency would be related to assertiveness. Fluency was measured by absence of fillers *(uhm, well, like, you know)* and ratio of clauses finished to clauses started. There were no statistically significant sex differences in these dimensions. [See II-A, IV-A, IV-D.]

C. Speech Disturbances

GARAI, JOSEF E., and AMRAM SCHEINFELD.
"Sex Differences in Mental and Behavioral Traits." *Genetic Psychology Monographs*, 77 (1968), 169-299.

Many studies report females to have superior language abilities of various sorts. Girls have better articulation than boys, and all speech disturbances, such as stuttering or poor articulation, aphasia and dyslexia, are much more frequent among males of all ages. Various reasons explaining female superiority are suggested; it may be that genetic factors produce more speech defects in boys. [*See VIII-A, VIII-B.*]

KRAMER, CHERIS.
"Women's Speech: Separate But Unequal?" *Quarterly Journal of Speech,* 60 (Feb., 1974), 14-24. Reprinted in Barrie Thorne and Nancy Henley, *Language and Sex: Difference and Dominance.* Rowley, Mass.: Newbury House, 1975.

In the literature on the ratio of male to female stutterers, there is general agreement that there are more male stutterers than female. But there is disagreement about biological vs. social causes. Some scholars claim stuttering is a hereditary trait, but "recent studies indicate that a male is more likely to stutter than a female because our culture places more importance on speech fluency in males than speech fluency in females. There is more pressure to speak well, and consequently the male feels more insecurity about his speech" (p. 6). (She cites Ronald Goldman, "Cultural Influences on the Sex Ratio in the Incidence of Stuttering," *American Anthropologist,* 69 [1967], 78-81.) [*See I, II-B, III-A, III-B-2, IV-A, IV-C.*]

McCARTHY, DOROTHEA.
"Some Possible Explanations of Sex Differences in Language Development and Disorders." *Journal of Psychology,* 35 (1953), 155-160.

There are small but important differences favoring girls, in "practically all aspects of language development which show developmental trends with age" among white American children, from the age of onset of true language. Boys more frequently suffer language disorders, particularly stuttering and reading disabilities; perhaps 65-100% of such disorders occur among boys. The differences appear at such an early age that their roots must be in early infancy, and there are enough environmental differences that genetic ones need not be postulated. (1) The early home environment is more satisfying to the girl infant, who can identify with and imitate the mother's speech, than to the boy, who needs to identify with and imitate the father's speech. Echo-reaction in girls will be closer to mother's speech, in any case, than boys' will be to father's speech, since the father's voice is much deeper. This stage, then, will be less satisfying for boys, even confusing, perhaps fear-producing. (2) If girls are as much preferred as natural children as they are as adoptive ones, they are more welcomed in the family and treated with more warmth. Boys suffering from insecurity and rejection in the home may be prone to later language disorders. (3) Sex role prescriptions separate boys from adult linguistic skills—they are sent outside to play, are not in as close range to the mother as girls. They hear less adult speech, and get less practice, both for this reason and because of the dissatisfaction (above) associated with echo-reaction. Girls not only have these advantages, but their typical toys have "high conversation value" and, in echoing the mother, they are likely to stimulate more conversation from her, and enter into a conversational relationship. Girls with language disorders always have a severely disturbed relationship with the mother. Boys' problems with language are intensified on entering school where a woman teacher, identified with the mother, awaits and pressures abound around language skills and competition with girls. [*See VIII-A.*]

IX. NONVERBAL ASPECTS OF COMMUNICATION

Findings of sex differences in nonverbal communication, in the literature of the several disciplines that investigate it, are not uncommon. However, they've largely been simply reported and left unexplored. Most of the articles cited below are ones that have focused in some way on sex differences, either through original research or theory, or through reviewing others' research. The subsections use some of the more common categories for dividing up the field, but it should be noted that this section might have many of the same divisions of the portion on language and speech. For instance, general ability in nonverbal communication, women's and men's nonverbal languages, and nonverbal conversational patterns are all possible topics at this stage of our knowledge, though the section concentrates on the nonverbal equivalent of "sex differences in word choice, syntactic usage, and language style" (section II-B). With further advances in research and theory, future topics could be the sexism in the nonverbal gesture system (e.g., the female-excluding handshake, obscene gestures), nonverbal language acquisition, nonverbal aspects of multilingual situations, and so on.

A. Comprehensive Sources

BIRDWHISTELL, RAY.
> "Masculinity and Femininity as Display." In *Kinesics and Context.* Philadelphia: Univ. of Pennsylvania Press, 1970, pp. 39-46.

Birdwhistell begins with a discussion of gender behavior, noting an increasing realization that "intragender and intergender behavior throughout the animal kingdom is not simply a response to instinctual mechanisms but is shaped, structured, and released both by the ontogenetic experience of the participating organisms and by the patterned circumstances of the relevant environment." When different animal species are rated on a spectrum by the extent of their sexual dimorphism, on the basis of secondary sexual characteristics human beings are relatively close to the unimorphic end. Such "weakly dimorphic species necessarily organize much of gender display and recognition at the level of position, movement, and expression." Informants from seven different societies could distinguish male movement from female movement, and interpreted the differences as instinctually and biologically based. Birdwhistell discusses "inappropriate" gender display, behavior in context (and the absence of any single message indicative of homosexuality), gender display in relation to division of labor, and the learning of gender display by the young in an age of rapid social change. [*See IX-D, IX-F.*]

FRIEZE, IRENE HANSON.
> "Nonverbal Aspects of Femininity and Masculinity Which Perpetuate Sex-Role Stereotypes." Paper presented at Eastern Psychological Association, 1974. (Frieze is at Dept. of Psychology, Univ. of Pittsburgh.)

Certain nonverbal behaviors are associated with dominance and status, others with liking and warmth; the same behaviors also differentiate men and women, in ways that perpetuate sex-role stereotypes. That is, males display more dominance and high status cues, and females indicate greater emotional warmth nonverbally. A behavior associated with dominance and high status, and with males, is control of greater territory and personal space, including a greater tendency to touch. Nonverbal behaviors associated with liking or warmth are also associated with women, and with lower status, suggesting that women's characteristic warmth and expressiveness are necessitated by their submissive roles. Higher status individuals show less direct eye contact, while women show more social eye contact. Women smile more than men; if the smiling is for other purposes than happiness or greetings, it would be another example of communication of low status. Women's greater receptivity to others' nonverbal cues, while supporting the stereotype of greater emotional warmth, may be necessary for their survival, as with other low status groups (blacks have been shown to be better than whites at interpreting others' nonverbal signals). "Clearly women communicate low status and submission, often unconsciously, through their use of 'feminine' nonverbal cues. Such behavior, although quite possibly caused originally by their lower status in our society, also serves to perpetuate sex-role stereotypes and lower status for women." The behaviors are difficult to confront since they are largely unconsciously emitted and interpreted. Women who are conscious of them are put in the position of having to choose between "feminine" and assertive behavior [on this point, see also references to Lakoff, especially V]. [See IX-C.]

HENLEY, NANCY M.

"Power, Sex, and Nonverbal Communication." *Berkeley Journal of Sociology*, 18 (1973-74), 1-26. Reprinted in Barrie Thorne and Nancy Henley, *Language and Sex: Difference and Dominance*. Rowley, Mass.: Newbury House, 1975.

The minutiae of everyday life (e.g., personal space, eye contact, touching, interrupting) are examined in the context of their contribution to social control, as micropolitical acts serving to maintain and perpetuate hierarchical social structure and to intimidate those who would change it. Women are particularly affected by subtle verbal and nonverbal cues because of their socialization to docility, their physical integration around centers of power, and their greater sensitivity to nonverbal communication. Much nonverbal behavior is not innate but culturally learned and designed to emphasize sex differences. Some 30 studies, both empirical and analytical, using both observational and experimental techniques, are reviewed, as well as a number of essays, to support and illustrate the discussion. Sex differences in language usage tend to put women at a disadvantage; there is also misogyny in much linguistic convention. Men talk more and probably interrupt more. There are sex and status differences in self-disclosure, and status differences in terms of address, the structure of which serves as a model for discussion of several nonverbal behaviors. In the nonverbal realm all the following are associated with higher status and with men: freedom of demeanor, greater personal space, freedom to touch others, staring, and withholding of personal information (particularly about emotions). Men's greater touching of women cannot be explained by sexual attraction, because that explanation would require women to touch men equally. Touch is analogous to the use of first name: used reciprocally, it indicates intimacy; nonreciprocally, it indicates status. Staring, pointing, touching, and interrupting are dominance gestures; lowering or averting the eyes, hesitating or stopping action or speech, cuddling to the touch, allowing interruption, and smiling are submission gestures, all more common to women than to men. There is a pattern of reaction to women's appropriation of the correlates of status (male gestures) which attributes them to sexual invitation. Many of these gestures, e.g., touching, staring, proximity, and relaxed demeanor, have a dual nature in that they are used between intimates, and therefore lend themselves well to sexual interpretation that denies women's assertion of power. Though manipulating these status cues will not change fundamental power relationships in the society, knowledge of them will raise consciousness and help people change those relationships.

HENLEY, NANCY, and JO FREEMAN.
   "The Sexual Politics of Interpersonal Behavior." In Jo Freeman, ed., *Women: A Feminist Perspective.* Palo Alto, Ca.: Mayfield, 1975.

This paper covers much of the same ground as "The Politics of Touch" (*see IX-E*) and "Power, Sex, and Nonverbal Communication" (above), in a less academic vein than the latter, with more detailed attention to the nitty gritty. Topics are: the sexist environment, initiation of sexual activity, demeanor, posture, clothing, self-disclosure, caring, personal space, touching, eye contact, verbal dominance, gestures of dominance and submission, language, and interpretation of women's violation of sex status norms.

JOHNSON, KENNETH R.
   "Black Kinesics–Some Nonverbal Communication Patterns in the Black Culture." *Florida FL Reporter,* Spring/Fall, 1971, 17-20+.

The existence of Black English has been conclusively demonstrated and described, and it can be expected that nonverbal communication patterns in the black culture also differ from those in the dominant culture. Black dialect is believed to have been influenced by the former African languages of black speakers; similarly, black nonverbal communication patterns may be related to African origins, as well as to blacks' isolation from the dominant culture. Differences in eye behavior and posture are described in detail to illustrate Black-white differences, and male-female differences among blacks, particularly in encounters with authority or in courtship. [*See IX-D, IX-F.*]

MEHRABIAN, ALBERT.
   Nonverbal Communication. Chicago: Aldine Atherton, 1972.

This book is a review of the extensive research of Mehrabian and his associates in identifying, describing, and classifying variables in nonverbal behavior. "Some of the most consistent findings about individual differences in implicit communication," he writes, "were related to sex differences" (p. 133), and he reports on these findings repeatedly in the book. He develops a three-dimensional framework which has the major factors of positiveness, potency (including dominance-submissiveness and status), and responsiveness, and interprets most of the findings relative to women in terms of the positiveness factor, relating them to other findings of greater affiliation and approval-seeking in females. Females are also seen to be more submissive in their nonverbal behaviors. [*See also IX-B, C, D, F, G.*]

O'CONNOR, LYNN.
"Male Dominance: The Nitty-Gritty of Oppression." *It Ain't Me Babe,* June 11-July 1, 1970, 9-11. Part of her essay, "Male Supremacy," reprint available from KNOW, Inc., P.O. Box 86031, Pittsburgh, Pa. 15221.

O'Connor compares animal gestures of dominance and submission with gestures between men and women, e.g., the direct stare, "presenting," effects of physical features. Submission in women is conveyed by averting the eyes, lowering or turning the head, smiling. "Charm is nothing more than a series of gestures (including vocalizations) indicating submission." Dominance gestures used by women result in several outcomes: re-establishment of control (through the use of depression or neuroticism) by the "submissive" man, heavy taming campaigns by aggressive men (through tyranny or temporary admiration), labelling as bitches and shrews, loss of job (domestic or paid), and general punishment. This analysis is presented in the context of male supremacy in society, which establishes the economic dependency of women on men and provides the backdrop against which the nitty-gritty of oppression occurs in the one-to-one relationship.

B. General Nonverbal Behavior

MEHRABIAN, ALBERT.
Nonverbal Communication. Chicago: Aldine Atherton, 1972.

In an experiment where subjects were observed while waiting with a stranger of the same sex, females were seen to be more affiliative (a composite measure), intimate (involving both body orientation and distance) and submissive (judged from body relaxation) (p. 154). In the matter of general ability in nonverbal communication, Mehrabian cites two studies that found no sex differences in ability to encode or decode moods (pp. 136-137). He reports his own study in which females were better able to convey and to interpret variations in like/dislike than males were. Male encoders were better able to communicate positive attitudes, and females were better at negative attitudes. A person's ability to communicate variations in negative attitude largely accounted for overall attitude-communicating ability; Mehrabian points out that our culture discourages explicit verbalization of negative feelings, thus the greater importance of the "implicit" channels of communication to express them. Furthermore, females' better encoding ability with negative attitudes is explained by males' "greater latitude to express negative feelings explicitly" (pp. 141-146). [*See IX-A, C, D, F, G.*]

ROSENTHAL, ROBERT, DANE ARCHER, JUDITH H. KOIVUMAKI, M. ROBIN DiMATTEO, and PETER L. ROGERS.
"Assessing Sensitivity to Nonverbal Communication: the PONS Test." *Division 8 Newsletter* of the Division of Personality and Social Psychology of the American Psychological Association, January, 1974, 1-3. See also "Body Talk and Tone of Voice: the Language Without Words." *Psychology Today,* 1974 (Sept.), 8, No. 4, 64-68.

This is a continuation of the research by Rosenthal and his associates on effects of experimenters' expectations on subjects' responses (and teachers' expectations on students' performance), focussing more recently on nonverbal cues as the link between expectation and response. To develop a measure of nonverbal sensitivity (PONS = Profile of Nonverbal Sensitivity), they made film clips of 220 segments of acted-out performances. There were 20 different scenarios, with variations on the positive/negative affect dimension and the submissive/dominant dimension. The film visual portion showed face, torso, both, or neither (auditory portion only). The audio track was manipulated so that subjects heard no sound, or heard either randomly scrambled voice (acoustical properties retained) or content-filtered voice (acoustical properties and intonation patterns retained) with each of the four visual conditions. Subjects who saw and/or heard the film clips were asked to choose the best description of the scene portrayed, and were judged for their "accuracy" in matching the intent of the actor. These early findings report on nearly 100 samples of subjects from North America, Europe, the Middle East, Australia, New Guinea, and East Asia, varying widely in age, education, cultural background, professional training, and mental health. In 75-80% of the samples, females performed slightly better than males. Female superiority held at all seven grade levels tested (from grade five through college), though the difference decreased with age. (The original film clips were made with a female actor, but when a partial version of the test was made with a male actor, female subjects still performed better). Among Americans, subjects were inaccurate at estimating their own PONS scores, though their spouses were fairly accurate at judging their (the subjects') sensitivity. In one group of teachers it was found that those more sensitive to nonverbal communication scored as less authoritarian and more democratic in teaching orientation, on another scale. Females were relatively better than males at interpreting negative affect; Rosenthal, et al. acknowledge that this superiority "may have had survival value." (It's also interesting to note that subjects retained 68% accuracy even when the film was speeded up to 1/24 of a second, indicating the extreme alertness with which people respond to nonverbal cues.)

WEITZ, SHIRLEY.
    "Sex Role Attitudes and Nonverbal Communication in Same and Opposite-Sex Interactions." Paper presented at American Psychological Association, 1974.

    Videotapes were made of 24 dyadic interactions of same- and mixed-sex pairs, cameras focused on the full body of each interactant separately. The subjects also filled out scales measuring sex role attitudes, dominance, and affiliation. The first minute of each interaction was analyzed for interpersonal warmth and dominance, without sound and without knowledge of the other in the dyad, by ten raters, and correlated with the attitude scales and sex of subject and of partner. Liberalism in sex role attitudes was significantly correlated with rated nonverbal warmth for men in both same-sex and opposite-sex interaction, i.e., men with liberal sex role attitudes were seen as warmer nonverbally, with both men and women, compared with men with conservative attitudes. (Women's nonverbal warmth was not significantly related to sex role attitudes, though Weitz reports a nonsignificant negative correlation between females' nonverbal warmth and liberalism in sex role attitudes, in same-sex interaction.) The rated nonverbal dominance for females was significantly negatively related to male dominance scale scores and rated female nonverbal warmth was significantly negatively related to male affiliation scores. Weitz suggests "a monitoring mechanism by which women adjust their nonverbal responses to the personality of the male in the interaction," creating "an equilibrium in the interaction which would result in maximum interpersonal comfort (especially for the male)." There was no significant relationship between females' nonverbal behavior and *female* partner scale scores, nor between male nonverbal ratings and partner scale scores. Females elicited warmer nonverbal responses from partners of either sex than did males, but women's nonverbal behavior was not rated as warmer than men's, contradicting earlier findings. Weitz emphasizes that these findings are from the first minute of interaction, and the dynamics of later interaction may reveal a different pattern; but the findings do present "a considerably more complex picture of sex differences in nonverbal communication than previous work which relied on the dominance=male, affiliation=female equation."

C. Use of Space

FRIEZE, IRENE HANSON.
   "Nonverbal Aspects of Femininity and Masculinity Which Perpetuate Sex-Role Stereotypes." Paper presented at Eastern Psychological Association, 1974. (Frieze is at Dept. of Psychology, Univ. of Pittsburgh.)

Control of greater territory and personal space is a behavior associated with dominance and high status, and with males (and exhibits a similar pattern in animals). One study reports that women are less likely to have a special and unviolated room in the home, others show that people tend to stand closer to women than to men, or to disturb women's path in crossing a street. Frieze also suggests that fathers often have a "special chair," and that men take up disproportionately more space than women in a double bed. Touching is another violation of personal space; women tend to be touched more, and men to do more touching [See IX-E]. Since these space relationships are associated with both status and sex, "controlled studies are needed to test the proposition that even when occupational status is controlled for, women occupy smaller and/or less desirable space." [See IX-A.]

LOTT, DALE F., and ROBERT SOMMER.
   "Seating Arrangements and Status." Journal of Personality and Social Psychology, 7 (1967), 90-95.

This article reports four studies, three questionnaire and one experimental, of how a subject would locate her/himself with regard to a person of higher, lower, or equal status, and of either sex. The first two studies, having 224 male and female university students (exact numbers for each sex not controlled, and not reported), reported significant sex differences. Both studies, in which paper-and-pencil diagrams of rectangular tables were used, showed a clear association of the "head" position (either extreme) with the higher status figure. When subjects designated the seat they would take on arriving first, and the seat the other would then take, "Approximately twice as many females as males sat side by side, and this is more frequent vis-à-vis a low-status than a high-status person." When subjects were asked to name the seat the other would take on arriving first, they tended to place all others at an "end" (of long side) chair, and this tendency was significantly greater for a high-status *male* authority figure. The authors further report: "It is also interesting that 37 subjects chose the head chair for themselves vis-à-vis Professor Susan Smith while half that number chose it vis-à-vis Professor Henry Smith."

MEHRABIAN, ALBERT.
   Nonverbal Communication. Chicago: Aldine Atherton, 1972.

   Mehrabian cites studies with the findings that females assume closer positions to others than males do; that female pairs take closer positions to each other than male pairs do; and that others assume closer positions to females than to males (all these are interpreted as females' expression of positive attitudes, and others' reciprocation of them) (pp. 133-134). Another study found male/female pairs to sit closest, then female/female, then male/male (pp. 20-21). [*See IX-A, B, D, F, G.*]

PIERCY, MARGE.
   Small Changes. New York: Doubleday, 1973.

   In this novel, a female character is teaching movement to a theater group: "Wanda made them aware how they moved, how they rested, how they occupied space. She demonstrated how men sat and how women sat on the subway, on benches. Men expanded   into available space. They sprawled, or they sat with spread legs. They put their arms on the arms of chairs. They crossed their legs by putting a foot on the other knee. They dominated space expansively. Women condensed. Women crossed their legs by putting one leg over the other and alongside. Women kept their elbows to their sides, taking up as little space as possible. They behaved as if it were their duty not to rub against, not to touch, not to bump a man. If contact occurred, the woman shrank back. If a woman bumped a man, he might choose to interpret it as a come-on. Women sat protectively using elbows not to dominate space, not to mark territory, but to protect their soft tissues." (p. 438).

SILVEIRA, JEANETTE.
   "Thoughts on the Politics of Touch." *Women's Press* (Eugene, Ore.), 1 (Feb., 1972), 13.

   Silveira observes that women are expected to walk around men in passing on the street, and reports an observational study that supports it: in 12 out of 19 man-woman pairs approaching each other on the street, women moved out of men's way (in four cases both moved, and in three the man moved). She comments on touching and smiling, and discusses the importance of changing power signals between men and women. [*See IX-G.*]

WILLIS, FRANK N., JR.
   "Initial Speaking Distance as a Function of the Speakers' Relationship." *Psychonomic Science,* 5 (1966), 221-222.

   Forty experimenters (members of a course) carried tape measures and, when approached by anyone, remained still and measured the inter-nose distance when the approacher began speaking. Sex of the listener-experimenter was found to be the most influential variable: women were approached more closely than men, by both men and women. Relationship of the two (stranger, acquaintance, etc.) had different effects on the different-sex approachers: "women stand quite close to good friends when speaking but stand back from ... friends." Women speakers approached closest to close friends, next closest to acquaintances, and stood farthest from friends, while men stood closest to friends and about equally distant from acquaintances and close friends.

D. Posture and Movement

ANONYMOUS.
"Exercises for Men." *Willamette Bridge* (date unknown). Reprinted in *Radical Therapist*, 1, No. 5 (1971), 15.

This is a short six-point piece, with illustrations, detailing some of the awkwardness of the prescribed public postures allowed to women: (1) "Sit down in a straight chair. Cross your legs at the ankles and keep your knees pressed together . . . " (2) "Bend down to pick up an object from the floor. Each time you bend remember to bend your knees so that your rear end doesn't stick up, and place one hand on your shirtfront to hold it to your chest. . . . " (3) "Run a short distance, keeping your knees together. You'll find you have to take short, high steps . . . " (4) "Sit comfortably on the floor. . . . Arrange your legs so that no one can see [your underwear]. Sit like this for a long time without changing position." (5) "Walk down a city street . . . Look straight ahead. Every time a man walks past you, avert your eyes and make your face expressionless. . . . " (6) "Walk around with your stomach pulled in tight, your shoulders thrown back, and your chest out. . . . Try to speak loudly and aggressively in this posture."

BIRDWHISTELL, RAY.
"Masculinity and Femininity as Display." In *Kinesics and Context*. Philadelphia: Univ. of Pennsylvania Press, 1970, pp. 39-46.

Birdwhistell gives some American examples of leg angle and arm-body angle, pelvic angle (roll) and facial expression. American females "when sending gender signals and/or as a reciprocal to male gender signals" bring the legs together; males typically separate the legs by a 10-15 degree angle. Female gender presentation has the upper arms close to the trunk, while male gender presentation moves the arms 5-10 degrees away from the body. Females may present the entire body from neck to ankles as a moving whole, whereas the male moves the arms independent of the trunk, and may subtly wag his hips. The male tends to carry his pelvis rolled slightly back, the female, slightly forward. [*See IX-A, IX-F.*]

JOHNSON, KENNETH R.
"Black Kinesics—Some Nonverbal Communication Patterns in the Black Culture." *Florida FL Reporter*, Spring/Fall, 1971, 17-20+.

The "black walk" of young black males—a slow stroll, casual and rhythmic, head slightly elevated and tipped to the side, one arm swinging with hand slightly cupped, the other arm limp or tucked in the pocket, thumb out—communicates the message of masculine authority (as does the young white males's walk). With the added message that "the young black male is beautiful," it beckons female attention to his sexual prowess, and communicates that he is "cool." In dealing with authority, when it's used in walking away from a reprimand it indicates the reprimand has been rejected. Young black females communicate rejection of authority by pivoting quickly on both feet, sometimes with a raising of the head and twitching of the nose, and walking briskly away. In courting, black males use a "rapping stance" which is a kind of stationary form of the "black walk"—at a slight angle to the female, head slightly elevated and tipped toward the female, eyes about ¾ open, weight of the body on the back heel, and arms as in the black walk. (The young white male rapping stance backs the female up against the wall, the YWM leaning toward her, one palm against the wall for support, and all his weight on the foot closest to the female; "sometimes, both arms are extended to support his weight, thus trapping the female between his two extended arms.") The young black female listens to the black male's rap nonchalantly, hand on hip. This stance in any situation communicates intense involvement, and in situations other than courtship communicates hostility and negative feelings toward the speaker. It is the black female's most aggressive stance, and is characterized by feet placed firmly in a stationary step, weight on the rear heel, buttocks protruded, one hand on the extended hip with fingers spread or in a fist. It may be accompanied by a slow rock, rolfing the eyes, and twitching the nose. Chicano females communicate the same message with both hands on hips, feet spread wide, head slightly raised. [See IX-A, IX-F.]

MEHRABIAN, ALBERT.
    Nonverbal Communication. Chicago: Aldine Atherton, 1972.

    Female communicators have more immediate orientation to the addressee than male communicators do (pp. 28, 65, 81); females oriented to face a liked addressee more directly than a disliked one, though males did the reverse when feelings were intense (p. 55). Males assumed more symmetric leg positions and more reclining positions, and had higher leg and foot movement rates than females (pp. 69-70). For females, but not males, a decrease in the trunk-swivel rate correlated with persuasiveness (p. 68). Males are generally more relaxed than females (pp. 14, 134), and communicators are more relaxed with females than with males (as communicators also are more relaxed with lower status addressees) (pp. 27-28). Females are said to "convey more submissive attitudes by characteristically assuming less relaxed postures in social situations" (p. 30). Males showed less body relaxation and greater vigilance toward an intensely disliked male addressee than did females (to the same), a finding Mehrabian attributes to the greater threat posed to the males (p. 101). [See IX-A, B, C, F, G.]

MEHRABIAN, ALBERT, and JOHN T. FRIAR.
    "Encoding of Attitude By a Seated Communicator Via Posture and Position Cues."
    Journal of Consulting and Clinical Psychology, 33 (1969), 330-336.

    Subjects (24M, 24F) were asked to imagine themselves in situations involving different kinds of addressees (liked/disliked, higher/lower status, male/female), and to sit in ways in which they would if they were actually interacting with them. The most important variables for the communication of positive attitude were found to be small backward lean of torso, close distance, and more eye contact; there was less sideways lean and more eye contact in communications with high-status addressees; and for females, less arm openness is an indicator of higher status of the addressee. Orientation: Both male and female subjects oriented farther away from an addressee of the opposite sex; females' leg orientation was farther from the addressee than was males'. Openness: Females showed less arm openness to high-status addressees than to low-status ones (males didn't differentiate); the mean degree of leg openness of male encoders was greater than that of female encoders. Relaxation: Torso lean was more backward for disliked addressees than for liked, and torso lean of male subjects was farther back than that of females.

E. Touching

HENLEY, NANCY M.
"The Politics of Touch." Paper presented at American Psychological Association, 1970. In Phil Brown, ed., *Radical Psychology*. New York: Harper & Row, 1973, pp. 421-433. Reprint available from KNOW, Inc., P.O. Box 86031, Pittsburgh, Pa. 15221.

Women are constantly kept in their place by many "little" reminders of their inferior status: the sexist environment, language, nonverbal communication. Verbal putdowns to halt a woman in intellectual discussion or anger are disguised as humor or compliments; veiled physical threats are similarly disguised. Anecdotal and descriptive analysis are offered suggesting that touching is a gesture of dominance often used by males on females. An observational study was made of who initiated touch among people in public: men touched women much more than vice versa, and touch between men and between women was about equal. That touch is a status sign is supported by findings that persons of higher socio-economic status more often touched those of lower status, and older persons more often touched younger, than vice versa. The few psychological studies that have been made on touch report females being touched more than males. The hypothesis that men's touching is sexually motivated is discussed and rejected. Touch has a dual nature (as do other behaviors, such as calling someone by first name) in that it can be used to indicate intimacy (in mutual usage) or status (nonmutual usage, toucher has higher status). Women's initiation of touching is often interpreted as a sexual advance. Men should guard against using touch to assert authority, especially with women, and change their reactions to being touched by women; women should refuse influence by touch, and become more assertive tactually when appropriate, though these actions themselves will not change the basic male chauvinist nature of male-female interaction.

HENLEY, NANCY M.
"Status and Sex: Some Touching Observations." *Bulletin of the Psychonomic Society*, 2 (1973), 91-93.

This is a straighter version, with additional data, of "The Politics of Touch" (above). Among same-age white adults, women's *non*reciprocation of men's touch was significantly greater than men's nonreciprocation of women's, and nonreciprocation by younger persons of the touch of older ones was significantly greater. When public settings were categorized as either indoor or outdoor, the sex differences in touching showed up more clearly in the outdoor settings, with little difference indoors.

JOURARD, SIDNEY M.
"An Exploratory Study of Body-Accessibility." *British Journal of Social and Clinical Psychology*, 5 (1966), 221-231.

A body-accessibility questionnaire was given to over 300 male and female unmarried students, asking what areas of the body were seen and/or touched by parents and closest friends of each sex, and what areas of the body of parents and friends the respondents saw and/or touched. Males reportedly touched fewer regions of their mothers' bodies than were touched by their mothers, and were not touched by mothers on as many regions as were females. Females exchanged physical contact on more areas of the body with their fathers than did males. The degree of accessibility of the different regions of the body was similar for the two sexes. Intercorrelations among the respondents' being-touched scores for different regions were higher for females than males, suggesting either more consistency about body accessibility, or "less discrimination . . . in accepting or spurning the extended hand of others."

JOURARD, SIDNEY, M., and JANE E. RUBIN.
  "Self-Disclosure and Touching: A Study of Two Modes of Interpersonal Encounter and Their Inter-Relation." *Journal of Humanistic Psychology,* 8 (1968), 39-48.

A body-contact questionnaire (see above) and self-disclosure questionnaire were given to 84 female and 54 male unmarried students, asking about parents, same-sex, and opposite-sex friends. Women and men showed similar patterns for physical contact except in relation to their fathers, whom the women touch more and are touched more by than the men. Women's mean total being-touched score was higher than men's. For women, opposite-sex friend reportedly touched them the most, but for the men, opposite-sex friend touched the least of the four target persons.

MONTAGU, ASHLEY.
  Touching: The Human Significance of the Skin. New York: Columbia Univ. Press, 1971. (New York, Harper & Row, 1972.)

"Sexual differences in cutaneous behavior," writes Montagu, "are very marked in probably all cultures" (p. 241). He states that females are "more apt to indulge in every sort of delicate tactile behavior than males," are more sensitive to tactile properties of objects, do more fondling and caressing, and are more gentle in approach on every level. "Backslapping and handshake crushing are specifically masculine forms of behavior," he (needlessly) informs us (p. 241).

TUAN, N.D., RICHARD HESLIN, and MICHELE L. NGUYEN.
  "The Meaning of Four Modes of Touch as a Function of Sex and Body Area." Available from Richard Heslin, Department of Psychological Sciences, Purdue University, W. Lafayette, IN 47907.

In this questionnaire study, students rated their agreement that certain meanings could be attributed to touch applied to certain areas of the body. The possible meanings assigned were playfulness, warmth/love, friendship/fellowship, sexual desire, and pleasantness. The touch modalities were pat, stroke, squeeze, or brush. The subjects, 41 male and 40 female unmarried undergraduates, were asked, "What does it mean when a (close) person of the opposite sex [not a relative] touches a certain area of my body in a certain manner?" They indicated their agreement on a four-point scale. Subjects were in general agreement that touch conveys warmth/love and is pleasant; "sexual desire" is the least likely interpretation given to touch, except that to "sexual" body areas (and males and females agreed on the areas associated with sexual desire). Analysis of variance for each meaning category showed an interaction of sex of subject and body area rated, indicating disagreement between the sexes about the meanings of touch to different areas. For males, pleasantness, sexual desire, and warmth/love formed a cluster; for females, touch that signified sexual desire was *opposed* to pleasantness, love/warmth, friendliness, and playfulness. The researchers compared their questionnaire responses to published reports on the skin sensitivity of various areas of the body, and found, in general, no significant relationship, except that body areas ranking high on sexual desire (and pleasantness, for males) alsò have high thresholds, i.e., are relatively insensitive. Females discriminate between their body areas more than males do, for touch; males, on the other hand, are more attuned to touch modalities than women. The authors interpret the differences only briefly, as a possible result of the sexual double standard and/or women's vulnerability to exploitation; and question whether the same results would be obtained from married women or non-college-student women (the women of this study are implicitly seen as the deviants).

F. Eye Behavior and Eye Contact

ARGYLE, MICHAEL, MANSUR LALLJEE, and MARK COOK.
   "The Effects of Visibility on Interaction in a Dyad." *Human Relations,* 21 (1968), 3-17.

A series of three experiments was performed in which visibility was varied for both members of a dyad, and measures of speech production and reported comfort, knowledge of others' reactions, and desire for more information were made. Females were uncomfortable if they could not see the other person when invisible themselves, which was not the case with male subjects. With reduced visibility males talked more and females less in a male-female pair; regardless of concealment, males seemed motivated to dominate and did so largely by interrupting and talking more. Females, especially when talking to males, felt "observed." [*See IV-D, IV-E.*]

ARGYLE, MICHAEL, and ROGER INGHAM.
   "Gaze, Mutual Gaze, and Proximity." *Semiotica,* 6 (1972), 32-49.

Three experiments are reported which examine the effect of distance on eye contact with relation to speaking, for males and females in both mixed- and same-sex dyads. Females seem to indicate intimacy by looking at the other when they themselves are talking; males indicate it by looking at the other while they are listening. There was less looking in male-female pairs than in either type of single-sex pairs. Also, when visibility was varied so that the subject saw the other through a one-way glass, females more than males tended to look more than in the normal, both-seeing condition; or, put another way, "females were more inhibited than males by the possibility of eye contact."

BIRDWHISTELL, RAY.
    "Masculinity and Femininity as Display." In *Kinesics and Context*. Philadelphia:
    Univ. of Pennsylvania Press, 1970, pp. 39-46.

According to Birdwhistell, males in American society are prohibited from moving the
eyeballs while the lids are closed, and generally should close and open their lids in a
relatively continuous movement. [*See IX-A, IX-D.*]

EXLINE, RALPH V.
    "Explorations in the Process of Person Perception: Visual Interaction in Relation to
    Competition, Sex, and Need for Affiliation." *Journal of Personality*, 31 (1963), 1-20.

Visual interaction was observed in 32 artificially-created three-person groups, half of
them all-male and half all-female. Women were found to engage in mutual visual interaction
(with each other) more than men, and sex was found to interact with affiliation need:
highly affiliative females look more at one another relative to less affiliative females than is
the case for males, who show the opposite tendency. Women's mutuality of looking was
greater when total looking was held constant. Competition seemed to inhibit mutual glances
among high affiliators and increase them among low affiliators, with women showing more
reaction to the situation than men. Women's visual activity is both more oriented toward
social stimuli than men's, and more affected by relevant social field conditions. Women have
also been found in some experiments to be more affected than men by visual cues in
establishing their bodily orientation in space, or in recognizing embedded figures; i.e., they
are "field dependent." Sex differences in eye contact may similarly be due to greater visual
dependence on objects in the social field.

EXLINE, RALPH, DAVID GRAY, and DOROTHY SHUETTE.
    "Visual Behavior in a Dyad as Affected by Interview Content and Sex of
    Respondent." *Journal of Personality and Social Psychology*, 1 (1965), 201-209.

Forty male and forty female college students were interviewed, half of each sex by a
male and half by a female interviewer. Women engaged in more mutual glances than did
men, and tended to look more at the interviewer while the latter was talking than did men,
particularly when instructed to conceal their feelings. Men, on the other hand, looked less
when told to conceal. All subjects gave much visual attention when the interviewer spoke
(more looking while listening than looking while speaking), regardless of other variables. The
data support an earlier finding of greater mutual glance among women than men, and
suggest also that women may maintain more eye contact regardless of the other's sex. The
data also suggest that sex differences in eye contact are a result of women's greater
orientation toward affectionate and inclusive relationships with others.

JOHNSON, KENNETH R.
    "Black Kinesics—Some Nonverbal Communication Patterns in the Black Culture."
    Florida FL Reporter, Spring/Fall 1971, 17-20+.

"Rolling the eyes," an expression of impudence and disapproval of someone in
authority, is more common among black females than among black males. It consists of

moving the eyes from one side of the socket to the other in a low arc (usually preceded by a stare at the other, but not an eye-to-eye stare), away from the other, with slightly lowered lids, and is very quick. The expression is mainly one of hostility, though it can also be used in general disapproval (as of another's uppity airs). [See IX-A, IX-D.]

MEHRABIAN, ALBERT.
    Nonverbal Communication. Chicago: Aldine Atherton, 1972.

Mehrabian cites his own and others' research with the following findings: females maintain more eye contact with others than males do; females tend to increase eye contact in positive interaction, while males decrease (both sexes decrease in aversive interaction) (p. 10). However, males showed more eye contact with extremely disliked males than with extremely disliked females (p. 101). In a persuasibility experiment, females speaking at the greater of two distances were more persuasive with greater eye contact than with less (90% vs. 50% contact), while males were more persuasive with less eye contact. [See IX-A, B, C, D, G.]

G. Smiling

Numerous feminists have made the observation that women engage in more smiling than men do, as appeasement and as a requirement of their social position, and perhaps further, out of fear and nervous habit. A survey of seven recent books on nonverbal communication (all of them by men), however, failed to uncover any statistics on the frequency of smiling or any recognitition of this difference which the women's movement regards as obvious and basic.

BUGENTAL, DAPHNE E., LEONORE R. LOVE, and ROBERT M. GIANETTO.
    "Perfidious Feminine Faces." *Journal of Personality and Social Psychology,* 17 (1971), 314-318.

Videotaped interactions of 20 families with "disturbed" children and 20 with "normal" ones, socioeconomically matched, were analyzed for parental facial expressions and verbal content: 81% of the children of the first group, and 86% of the second group, were boys. Fathers made more positive statements when smiling than when not smiling, but mothers' verbal messages were no more positive when smiling than when not. Mothers' verbal messages were more variable than fathers' verbal messages; there were no effects that were a function of child disturbance. Only 13% of the lower class mothers smiled more than once, whereas 75% of the middle class mothers smiled more than once (there was no significant difference between classes in fathers' smiling). Parents, particularly mothers, smiled often when observed, very little when supposedly unobserved. Earlier studies had found that children respond to women's smiles, in comparison with men's, as relatively neutral, and that they respond to contradictory messages (negative statement accompanied by a smile) as negative, and more so if the speaker is a woman. Since women use the smile as part of a culturally prescribed role, there may be little or no relationship between smiling and verbal message. The young child's response to a woman's smile is then seen as accurate, in the sense that her smile does not directly signal friendliness or approval.

CHESLER, PHYLLIS
   Women and Madness. New York: Doubleday, 1972.

   "Women, as well as men, are deeply threatened by a female who does not smile often enough and, paradoxically, who is not very unhappy. Women mistrust and men destroy those women who are not interested in *sacrificing* at least something for someone for some reason" (pp. 278-279).

FIRESTONE, SHULAMITH.
   The Dialectic of Sex. New York: Bantam Books, 1970.

   "The smile is the child/woman of the shuffle; it indicates acquiescence of the victim to his own oppression. In my own case, I had to train myself out of that phony smile, which is·like a nervous tic on every teenage girl. And this meant that I smiled rarely, for in truth, when it came down to real smiling, I had less to smile about. My 'dream' action for the women's liberation movement: *a smile boycott,* at which declaration all women would instantly abandon their 'pleasing' smiles, henceforth smiling only when something pleased *them*" (p. 90).

MEHRABIAN, ALBERT.
   Nonverbal Communication. Chicago: Aldine Atherton, 1972.

   In an experiment on persuasiveness, males' "facial pleasantness and activity" were judged to be less than those of females (p. 70). In a role-playing experiment, males increased their facial pleasantness when attempting to deceive, whereas females in the deception condition showed no more facial pleasantness than in the truthful condition (p. 88). [*See IX-A, B, C, D, F.*]

NIERENBERG, GERARD I., and HENRY H. CALERO.
   How to Read a Person Like a Book. New York: Hawthorn, 1971. (New York: Pocket Books, 1973.)

   Nierenberg and Calero cite a smile classification system of Ewan Grant (Birmingham University—reference not given), in which one of the five basic smiles is the "lip-in smile . . . often seen on the faces of coy girls." It is similar to another basic smile, the "upper, or how-do-you-do, smile," which has only the upper teeth showing and the mouth slightly open. In addition, in the lip-in smile, the lower lip is drawn in between the teeth. "It implies that the person feels in some way subordinate to the person she is meeting," quote the authors (Pocket edition, p. 32).

SILVEIRA, JEANETTE.
    "Thoughts on the Politics of Touch." *Women's Press* (Eugene, Ore.), 1 (Feb., 1972),
    13.

    Silveira cites smiling as a signal of submission, particularly from women to men, and compares this with its similar use among monkeys and apes. Women seem more apt to smile especially (1) when a woman and man are greeting each other, and (2) when the two know each other only moderately well. The smile indicates assurance that no harm or aggression is intended, rather than pleasure and friendliness. [*See IX-C.*]

RELEVANT WOMEN'S GROUPS

Caucuses, Committees, and Independent Groups in Disciplines Related to the Study of Sex Differences in Language, Speech, and Nonverbal Communication

[This list is not meant to be complete, but should be able to put readers in touch with the main and most active groups in a given field.]

Language and Linguistics
    Linguistic Society of America
        LSA Women's Caucus
            Correspondent: Lynette Hirschman
                           4709 Baltimore Avenue
                           Philadelphia, PA   19143

    Modern Language Association
        Women's Caucus of the MLA
            President: Dolores Barracano Schmidt
                           R. D. 3
                           Slippery Rock, PA   16057

        Committee on the Status of Women in the Profession
            c/o   Elaine Hedges
                           Towson State College
                           Baltimore, MD   21204

Sociology
    Sociologists for Women in Society
            Chairperson: Arlene Kaplan Daniels
                           Department of Sociology
                           Northwestern University
                           Evanston, IL   60201

Psychology
    Association for Women in Psychology
            Correspondent: Dorothy Camara
                           7012 Western Avenue
                           Chevy Chase, MD   20015

    American Psychological Association
        Division of Psychology of Women
            c/o   American Psychological Association
                           1200 Seventeenth Street, N. W.
                           Washington, DC   20036

Anthropology
American Anthropological Association
Committee on the Status of Women in Anthropology
1703 New Hampshire Avenue, N. W.
Washington, DC   20009

New York Women's Anthroplogy Conference
c/o   Constance Sutton
                            Department of Anthropology
                            New York University
                            25 Waverley Place
                            New York, NY   10003

Philosophy
Society for Women in Philosophy
c/o   Philosophy Department
                            University of Illinois, Chicago Circle
                            P. O. Box 4348
                            Chicago, IL   60680

American Philosophical Association
    Women's Caucus
        Chair: Mary Mothersill
                            Department of Philosophy
                            Barnard College
                            New York, NY   10027

Writing
Feminist Writers Workshop
c/o   Ruth Todasco
                            Loop Center YWCA
                            37 South Wabash Avenue
                            Chicago, Il   60603

Teachers of English
National Council of Teachers of English
    Committee on the Role and Image of Women in the Council and Profession
        Chair: Johanna S. DeStefano
                                200 Ramseyer Hall
                                The Ohio State University
                                Columbus, Ohio 43210

AUTHOR INDEX TO THE BIBLIOGRAPHY

This Bibliography is a part of a series of bibliographies sponsored by the American Sociology Association Section on Sex Roles. Other projected Bibliographies in the series are:

Barbara Babcock, Ann Freedman, Eleanor Holmes Norton, Susan Deller Ross, and Friends, Women and the Law: A Collection of Reading Lists, 1971

Margrit Eichler, An Annotated Selected Bibliography of Bibliographies on Women (in preparation).

Nancy Henley and Barrie Thorne, She Said/He Said: An Annotated Bibliography of Sex Differences in Language, Speech and Non-verbal Communication, 1975.

Carole Joffe, Patricia Bourne and Pamela Roby, Child Care Bibliography, 1974.

Rita Seiden Miller, The Social Aspects of Pregnancy: A Preliminary Bibliography, 1974.

Pamela Roby, Selected Bibliography on Prostitution, 1975.

They may be obtained from KNOW. Please send stamped, self-addressed envelope for further information to KNOW, Inc., P.O. Box 86031, Pittsburgh, PA 15221.

LANGUAGE AND SEX
Difference and Dominance

Edited by: Barrie Thorne, Ph. D. , sociolinguist at
Michigan State University
Nancy Henley, Ph. D. , psycholinguist at the
University of Lowell (Massachusetts)

A new comprehensive book on sexism and sex differences in language.
First in the new Series in Sociolinguistics from Newbury House Publishers. Series Editor: Roger Shuy, director of the sociolinguistics
program, Georgetown University. Available, Fall, 1975, in paper-
back, $8.95.

In Two Parts:

Part I   Readings: * Overview * Separate But Unequal Speech? *
A Nonsexist Dictionary * Speaker Sex: Sociolinguistic Variable * Se-
mantic Derogation of Women * Intonation * Class, Sex, and Language
Change * Interruption and Silence * Cross-Cultural Survey * Children's
Speech * Teacher-Child Interaction * Nonverbal Communication

        AUTHORS: Bodine -- Brend -- Cherry --
                Graham -- Henley -- Kramer --
                Sachs -- Schulz -- Swacker --
                Thorne -- Trudgill -- West --
                Zimmerman

Part II   Bibliography: The first fully annotated, interdisciplinary
bibliography in this important field. * Topically arranged * cross-
referenced * with author index * analysis and commentary by com-
pilers * readable and scholarly

Of special interest for: Courses in Linguistics, Speaking, English,
other language courses; Women's/Feminist Studies; Sociology;
Psychology; Education; Writing; and many others. Women's Groups --
Researchers -- Teachers -- Counselors -- Libraries -- Men's
Groups -- Women's Centers -- Feminists

                        -- Personal, Political, Linguistic Change --

NOTE FROM KNOW

The separate publication of SHE SAID/HE SAID, the annotated bibliography from the book LANGUAGE AND SEX: DIFFERENCE AND DOMINANCE, is the happy result of the energy of its authors, the cooperation of NEWBURY HOUSE PUBLISHERS and the faith of the KNOW Collective that business contracts can and should be mutually, equally beneficial.

The bibliography is a student's and scholar's tool and as such it should be readily, inexpensively and immediately at hand - a reference work you can carry in your pocket. It is this need that KNOW seeks to meet.

What makes this bibliography doubly valuable is that in addition to its usefulness, it is a delight to read. We think that the publisher of the entire work, LANGUAGE AND SEX: DIFFERENCE AND DOMINANCE will gain by KNOW's publication of SHE SAID/HE SAID because each copy of it is a compelling advertisement for the larger work.

We expect that reading the bibliography will lead you to decide that you <u>must</u> read the whole book! If it does, send $8.95 for: LANGUAGE AND SEX: DIFFERENCE AND DOMINANCE

edited by Barrie Thorne and Nancy Henley

to: NEWBURY HOUSE PUBLISHERS
68 Middle Road, Rowley, Massachusetts 01969

SHIPPING LABEL

_____

_____

_____

_____
(City)   (State)   ZIP!